MW00785735

Praise for Just Left

"Fierce and compassionate, bold and resolute, ~~~~~~ ~~~~~
Sun is at once a coming into consciousness as it ~~ ~ ~~~~ ~~~ ~~~
action by and for a new generation of Chamorr~~ ~~~ ~~~~~ ~~~~~~
of an island and archipelago long colonized ~~ ~~~~ ~~~~ ~~~ ~~~
United States of America. As critical towards ~~~~~ ~~~~~~ ~~~~~
and abet the colonizer as he is of the colonizers themselves, Aguon also
importantly situates the need for Native Struggles for Political and
Cultural Self-Determination and Sovereignty within Feminist/Womanist
critiques and global struggles for economic, social, and environmental
justice, thereby providing a glimpse into the possibilities for local
struggle informed and articulated to global movements beyond pan-
indigenous movements per se, and for keeping global movements and
political theory grounded in Indigenous traditions."

Dr. Vicente M. Diaz
Associate Professor of American Culture
University of Michigan, Ann Arbor

"Julian Aguon's work reminds readers that pure and potent colonialism
lives on, threatening the island of Guam with ever-more harmful forms
of American cultural, political, economic, and ecological disaster. The
passionate pages of this volume attempt to shake complacent, colonized
readers so that they might realize that the stakes are as high as ever
before in the face of American militarization and capitalist
globalization."

Dr. Anne Perez-Hattori
Assistant Professor of Pacific History and Humanistic Studies
University of Guam

The ocean is our home, Mother, inspiration; it will always be there for us. —alina alcoga

"...Aguon re-introduces us to the principles of international law as a guiding framework to the resolution of the dilemma brought about by the present non self-governing arrangements which provide the trappings of democratic governance, but in reality are rather democratically deficient by any objective examination. Indeed, an important component of new millennium colonialism is the existence, but not the recognition, of this democratic deficit...

...Just Left of the Setting Sun" should be required reading for the people in the remaining territories, young and old, who need to discover/re-discover the fire within, that they might further move the process forward, if only by a few steps further along the continuum. In a very real sense, as Aguon observes, "inside the heart of the Chamoru is still an ocean of latent potentialities waiting to surge."

Dr. Carlyle Corbin
Advisor on Governance and Political Development
St. Croix, Virgin Islands

Just Left

of

the Setting Sun

Julian Aguon

blue ocean press
tokyo

1898 Consciousness Studies Series
Guahan (Guam) - Philippine Islands - Puerto Rico - Cuba

Copyright © 2006 Julian Aguon

All rights reserved.
This publication may not be reproduced, stored in a retrieval system, or transmitted in any form or by any means, electronic, mechanical, photocopying, recording, or otherwise, without prior written permission of the publisher, except by a reviewer who may quote brief passages in a review to be printed in a periodical.

Published by:
blue ocean press, an Imprint of Aoishima Research Institute (ARI),
#807-36 Lions Plaza Ebisu, 3-25-3 Higashi, Shibuya-ku,
Tokyo, Japan 150-0011

mail@aoishima-research.com
URL: http://www.blueoceanpublishing.com
         http://www.aoishima-research.com

Cover Design by romeo carlos

The cover art is original art by Hoi Yin Chan, 1993, untitled. It is a pastel drawing done when she was in the seventh grade. Chan won a Guam Council on the Arts and Humanities Agency contest with this drawing.

ISBN: 978-4-902837-32-3

This book is funded in part by the National Endowment for the Humanities. Any views, findings, conclusions, or recommendations expressed in this project do not necessarily represent those of the National Endowment for the Humanities.

KONSEHILON
TINAOTAO
GUAM

GUAM
HUMANITIES
COUNCIL

DEDICATION

To the Chamoru People
who deserve good art
and Justice

and

To the Ancient Beauty
for Whom no words
can suffice.

Get your nerves together baby and set the record straight

- Nina Simone

Contents

The Emancipation of Morning

W aiting in the wings of the world of all that is yet to be said and step into the light of a real regard is Guahan, a place the international community knows almost nothing about. Of her there is lamentably much to say and even more that has been strategically stopped in the saying. Known to the outside world as Guam, she is the southernmost island of the Mariana Islands in the Western Pacific Ocean. One of the last remaining colonies of the United States (U.S.) and its most cruelly-kept secret, she moves in silence among the longest occupied territories in the world, the aching shard of a promise the twentieth century did not keep. Disfigured by four centuries of colonization, she is, at the dawn of the twenty-first one, hardly recognizable. She stares out at us listless like a woman grieving her lost beloved.

First to cast a colonial gaze on Guahan in the 1500s was Spain. By the next century its imperialistic claim to the homeland of the Chamoru was realized. Unspeakable havoc was wreaked upon the Chamorus after decades of foreign-inflicted disease and warfare, which were in turn exacerbated by internal conflicts: from Spain in the late 1600s to 1898, the year the U.S. signed the Treaty of Paris and took her from the Spanish; to 1941 when the U.S. abandoned her, leaving her open and defenseless to Japan's notorious three-year occupation; to 1944 when American boys came back blazing to re-stick their flag in her soil.[1] Now in agony on the cross of the American neo-imperialist project, she

---

1.   The U.S. left Guahan open and defenseless to Japanese forces in WWII. According to Chamoru scholar Anthony Leon Guerrero, "The island of Guam was not fortified to defend itself the days leading up to the War in the Pacific. In fact, the U.S. Government had no intention of defending Guam in the event of a war." In his essay, The Economic Development of Guam, published first in 1996 in The Political Status Education Coordinating Commission (2002). *Kinalamten Pulitikåt: Siñenten I Chamorro: Issues in Guam's Political Development: The Chamorro Perspective,* he argues that the U.S. re-occupation of Guahan was disastrous for the Chamoru people. "The American re-invasion began with intense, off-shore shelling...For thirteen days, U.S. Naval Ships pounded the island with hundreds of tons of bullets, bombs and shells. The villages of Agana, Sumay, Agat, Piti, Asan, Tumon, Tamuning and Yigo were obliterated." p. 90.

writhes with the knowledge that she must somehow, and against all odds, stay the hand of Empire again in this day. And it is late in the day.

The problem though is not merely that she has a war on her hands but that she is pitifully ill prepared to fight it. And this war is one the U.S. is waging quite masterfully on her people – a war so clever it is exacting the death of the native Chamoru under a malady whose name we have yet to learn.

As the project known as corporate globalization continues marching to the beat of deafening drums and continues deepening disparity among the poor of the world, it is also growing clearer in the collective imagination of the world's people, and thankfully more subject to a good fight. People moving in praxis, that synthesized space where theory meets action, are rising with resolve to the occasion. Folks across continents are busy exposing the working parts of what many of us concerned with the deepening divide between the rich and poor of the world call American Empire. Some have even succeeded. But as America's perilous push to dominate the global political stage is being forced to peel back its mask by thoughtful citizens the world over, we, the indigenous people of America's westernmost possession, are not joining in the fight. We are kept under lock and key. Cleverly invisible in the international community so that no one sees as we slip quietly into the sea. Not marching, but being marched, to the drums of our own disempowerment. But alone, that information is insufficient to understand the quality of anguish today being loosed on the Chamoru people.

Who are we anyway? Contrary to the general consensus of a generally uninformed global citizenry, we are not merely residents of one big military installation as much as the U.S. Department of Defense would have the outside world believe. We are more than just Natives of an island that has become an extension of the federal Department of Interior.[2] Chamorus are the indigenous people of the first island in the Pacific Ocean to make contact with the western world one March morning (insert mourning) in 1521. But our arms stretch back millennia before that. Migrating from the south coast of China more than four thousand years ago, our Austronesian forerunners pioneered the art of celestial navigation. The best archaeological and linguistic evidence indicates that the ancestors of the contemporary Chamoru purposefully sailed the *sakman* (outrigger sailing canoe) eastward into the land mass that became known in colonial times as the Mariana Island Chain and long before other Austronesians would come to populate the rest of Micronesia and Polynesia.[3] We ushered in the dawn of one of the largest-scale human migrations in history – the movement into the Pacific known as the migration of the Austronesian peoples into Oceania. We are the first in a long line that ends with those who populated the last islands in the ocean, Rapa Nui/Easter Island and Aotearoa/New Zealand.[4] We belong, quite literally, to one Oceanic family.

We were fisher folk with our own distinct calendar, which we rendered by the phases of the new moon. Our word for moon is *pulan*. Interestingly, this also means: to watch protectively over, like mother to child. This hints to a verity of our old ways: we organized our lives along deeply matrilineal lines. Clans, genealogies, and land tenure were all things held in the protective forearms of our women. More than this, we belonged to a matrilineal region. Save Yap and Kiribati, the Micronesian islands as a whole were women-centered.[5] But grievously, the hour of patriarchy fell on our lands and the colonial forces that came would prove incapable of understanding such things.

A heritage so real and worthy of pride is not the typical song we are singing these days. Coming home from college, it didn't take long to figure out just how far Chamoru people are being steered down waters of neo-colonialist policy.[6] Policy pulling us up by the roots. At the time this book goes to press, we Chamorus are being set out on a course that our

---

2.   In varied circles, there is an allusion to Guahan as a mere extension of the U.S. Department of Interior, suggesting that many people have already ascertained the truth that the people of Guahan are relatively powerless in the dominating scheme of things. I say "relatively powerless" not by virtue of being naïve about the ridiculously uneven power dynamics between the U.S. federal government and our own, but rather because of an awareness of a second, altogether separate sphere of power held in the hands of the oppressed themselves, one that can be articulated in the struggle to regain ourselves.

3.   Leonard Iriarte, personal interviews throughout 2005.

4.   Ibid.

5.   Teaiwa, Teresia (1992). Microwomen: US Colonialism and Micronesian Women Activists. Rubenstein, Donald, ed. *Pacific History: Papers from the 8th Pacific History Association Conference*. Mangilao, Guam: University of Guam and Micronesian Area Research Center. Pgs. 125-141.

current Governor believes will bring us to a glittering destination akin to a twinkle in the eye of our master. We have discovered that our legislature, perhaps the most august and weathered local institution in our turbulent political history, is largely losing its will. Home of some of the most courageous courses of action we've taken on the road to righting our relationship with the U.S., its light is waning. Our senators seem to be turning their faces away from the horizon of larger sociological questions that, once raised, would assail the apathy their politics profess.

Our political leaders are drawing newer lines in the sand. Our Governor and his friends, the local elite benefiting from the current

---

6.　　By neo-colonialist policy is meant those racist, capitalist paradigms dominating the global political stage, paradigms that uphold Profit as the King of Everything Else. In today's global political economy, neo-colonialism is most transparent in the workings of economic oppression, or the institutionalized depravity inherent in an unfettered global capitalist system. With weak restraints on the "free" market and no serious consideration of human rights and general well being of peoples, such a system is essentially colonialist. For more information about the colonialist nature of the global political economy, one can consult the many books published by South End Press of Cambridge, Massachusetts. In addition, some capable books include Oswaldo de Rivero's *The Myth of Development*, *The Case Against Free Trade: GATT, NAFTA, and the Globalization of Corporate Power* by Ralph Nader, David Philips, Pat Choate, as well as Scholar-Activist Vandana Shiva's various interviews and writings. It is worth noting that though the physical part of warfare has largely ended in our homeland, the spiritual, cultural, political, and economic elements of war has clearly not ended. Privatization as a prized political agenda is likewise essentially colonialist and a gross continuation of racist, oppressive, and profit-driven thought in Guahan. Further, Chamoru Sociologist Michael P. Perez, in Contested Sites: Pacific Resistance in Guam to U.S. Empire published in 2001 in *Amerasia Journal* 27:1, defines neo-colonialism in the following words:

> Neocolonialism refers to contemporary manifestations of older
> colonial conditions (i.e., political domination, cultural alteration
> and ideological justifications) under new guises. For instance,
> persistent U.S. neocolonial conditions involve political status
> and subordination, second-class citizenship, lack of control of
> in-migration, land acquisition, cultural erosion and
> Americanization. p. 100.

In the article, Perez goes on to assert: "Moreover, U.S. neocolonialist discourse advocates romanticized ideals of democracy and human rights, while violating and justifying the violation of those very principles."

arrangements, have set out on a road that suggests they have bought what they have been sold or merely see profit for themselves at hand, and are now trying to push us their Sell Everything agenda. They have taken an ideological stick and drawn some very harsh lines indeed. Those lines tell us that who we have been must now be separated from who we are to become. Already divided along the false lines of Democrat and Republican that fail small, oppressed communities such as ours, we are being busied in ever-pettier affairs, distracted by ever-smaller arguments. All so that we, they hope, lose sight of the bigger picture – that we are being co-opted in our own annihilation.

Today – as our International Financial Institutions including the World Trade Organization (WTO), the World Bank (WB) and the International Monetary Fund (IMF) remain deaf to the wailing, tender agonies of the Third World and continue praying at the neo-capitalist altar of the Washington Consensus, as privatization of essential infrastructure like water only heightens chaos in country after country, as the WB increases its funding for projects that have already proven failed experiments, as the WTO continues to betray the world's poorest people, in particular women, by rendering them and their work invisible in its "working" economic equations, as indigenous knowledge is being cleverly stolen by multinational corporations under the vulgar pretext of intellectual property, as the cradle of human spiritual history continues to be vandalized by vulgar irreligion, as Bush continues to malign the heart of the ancient world and advances his war on terror which is designed not to end, as the poor of America continue to pay, fight, and die for this war of insanity while the rich of America continue to shamefully benefit from it – we in Guahan are busy looking frightened and empty into a mirror in which our face does not even appear.

Today, here is how we are stacking up. Or rather, how we are not:

Local leaders and businessmen are trying to sell our homeland off in chunks under the guise of a pragmatic mass privatization agenda. First electricity and telecommunications, now water (and more is slated for the next round). The argument from the top-down is that the local people cannot do the job and that a private company, which will almost surely come from the U.S., would operate our water systems more efficiently. But we know. We know that water privatization is, globally, a $400 billion business.[7] Deals have been made. Contracts have been signed. Deep pockets have made friends of local leadership. People in powerful positions are considering 3,000 acres in one of our southern villages to build a ludicrous landfill. Again, we know. We know that their proposed site for this obstruction is directly over a rich water source, one our near future may prove we direly need. Not to mention that its construction will inevitably displace a historical site of ancient artifacts. The elite who control the conversation through the media are trampling on the integrity of a civilization they hope will barely be able to fight back. Assaulted daily by reportage that dispenses more propaganda than news and a newspaper in the business of crushing anything that reflects a pro-Chamoru position, the space for real dialogue is shrinking, as is our resolve.[8] So quick is the pace at which this Made-in-America mission is advancing, it is devouring the dialogue and choking the hope to elevate it. In such a depraved intellectual climate, it is no wonder that the machinations of our disempowerment are nothing short of dazzling.

But the band plays on and by some miracle, those able to penetrate the cloud and access information have figured out some important stuff, most importantly that we are being wronged. With bent backs, we are at home in our kitchens and living rooms engaging even our closest friends and families who have set their hearts on singing America. And we are beginning to understand. We no longer have the luxury of being *merely* at war with a colonizer; we are at war with internalized colonization, or second tier colonialism, first. We are not up against *merely* an outside power, but each other in a struggle of what it is we ultimately value. With increasing clarity, we are seeing that the war most immediate is that for our people's attention. The tragedy of our day,

---

7.   Marsden, Bill (2003, February 3) Cholera and the Age of the Water Barons [Electronic version]. *The Center for Public Integrity*, p. 3. It is important to note that according to this article, US$400 billion is the conservative estimate of what some believe is as high as US$3 trillion.

8.   By pro-Chamoru position I simply mean an ideological position consciously aligned with the restoration and affirmation of dignity among oppressed and disempowered Chamoru people who have yet to exercise their right to Self Determination and walk into the light of their long-denied freedom.

however, is that cynicism like a bad lover has come calling and many of us no longer believe this war is one we can win.

Maybe I am just stubborn. Or maybe I am just convinced that indigenous people everywhere concerned with the welfare of their communities have all come upon similar circumstance. When our histories have been held hostage for so long it should surprise no one that our journeys home will no doubt be long. But what the outside world should by now understand about indigenous people is that we are of a resilient stock. We bend in the wind; we do not break in it. We manage, maybe by the mysterious hand of the Almighty, to keep getting up, and always one more time than we are knocked over.

Our Oceanic sisters and brothers have given us some good models of preserving cultural integrity. Our partners in American colonization, the *kanaka maoli* of Hawaii (native Hawaiians), have given us an example of cultural revival that works – immersion schools at which children learn in their own tongue. And they took this from their kin in Aotearoa; I guess you could say the thing we still do well is share. Our brothers in the Caroline Islands in between, including, and surrounding Chuuk and Yap have given us an art the rest of us in the ocean lost –traditional seafaring skills. And the list goes on. Micronesia, Melanesia, Polynesia. Ocean peoples determined to emancipate their histories.

It's just that some of us are ahead of others. We here are way behind. But to understand how this internalized colonization came to so badly conquer the minds of the Chamoru people, one must first understand our history. The end of the last world war would be a good place to start.

In July and August of 1944, the bloodiest last months of the Japanese occupation of Guahan, the U.S. military dropped bombs on our paramount villages.[9] Much like the bombs that rain relentlessly on Iraq today, bombs fell on us in the name of saving us (but you can't say something like that here in Guahan and get away with it because the dangerously patriotic climate convulsing the continental U.S. post 9/11 is just as strong here, which only deepened a tragically patriotic post WWII attitude among our people). So on the eve of the same year the

9.   In Chamoru pre-history, *Hagåtña* was the paramount village of *I Manmatao*, or the *Matao*, the original word for our people. *Hagåtña* is in important ways our paramount village, as the seat of our government is there.

U.S. became one of the founding states of the United Nations (U.N.) and in New York lauded the principles of international law – including self determination and decolonization – it was busy here planning never to grant us those very things. As the words liberty and freedom found wings in the rhetoric of the international community that year, they sounded like trumpets over our ravaged island and we wept at the break of what we believed to be a new day. But in our case, the words fell like the bombs did. Heavy.

And we were recaptured. Amidst gunfire and cans of Spam and ill intentions. By the time the war ended, 70% of our island was in military hands, which was only the start of what would become the project some of us call The Radical Dispossession of The Chamoru.[10] After taking our land, the military closed our ports, shut us out politically and economically, and denied us the excitement stirring in the rest of the region, which already had decolonization on the brain. In the late 60s and early 70s as the former U.S. Trust Territory of Micronesia engaged in political status negotiations with the U.S., we watched as the region began walking the long road to decolonization. While our sisters and brothers forged new futures in the last two decades, becoming the Republic of the Marshall Islands, the Republic of Palau (Belau), the Federated States of Micronesia and the Commonwealth of the Northern Mariana Islands, we remained caught in an arm's length of space so crushingly lonely it is almost unimaginable. One slow foot forward after another, the U.S. gradually loosened its stranglehold on the neck of Micronesia and, at the behest of its international obligations, eventually let go. But even they are constrained by the U.S. imperialist project today through economic dependence on the U.S. and U.S. military interests in the region.[11] This, of course, is another story entirely. Our story here is one of mirrors and our facelessness in them. Of looking longingly at the outside world from a world under duress. While we watched the U.S. engage our Micronesian kin in status talk, we remained cloaked by a country that would consistently postpone our freedom, constraining us to the political and economic infancy under which we flay still.

---

10. Bettis, Leland (2002), Colonial Immigration in Guam in The Political Status Education Coordinating Commission (2002). *Kinalamten Pulitikåt: Siñenten I Chamorro: Issues in Guam's Political Development: The Chamorro Perspective.*

A national security clearance policy designed by the Department of Defense to give the military complete control over who came in and out of Guahan created a black hole of lost economic opportunities.[12] This in turn created a dependency on the U.S. at the heart of our most entangled affairs. The U.S. move to have exclusive control over our 200-mile Economic Exclusive Zone is undoubtedly tied to the fact that today we embarrassingly resort to importing most of our fish from outsiders. Unbelievably, fish taken from our waters are canned elsewhere and then sold to us. The U.S. use of immigration as a colonial tool to flood our homeland with foreigners to intentionally dilute our native population is a direct violation of international treaties and an affront to our dignity.[13] To date, we make up less than half our population and those of us who understand the rights vouchsafed to us by international law are now being told by our colonizer that a native-only vote of self-determination is racist and unconstitutional.[14] This defunct rationale could almost be laughable if it were not so lamentable.

In the same breath that we are measured against the U.S. Constitution, we are denied full protection and equality under it. We are a part of America apart. Our status as "Unincorporated Territory" reveals

---

11.   Teaiwa (1992). See also Oceania: Islands, Land, People by Geoffrey M. White and Lamont Lindstrom, in *Cultural Survival Quarterly: State of the Peoples*, from which the following quote is taken:

> Political independence has not been accompanied by economic independence. The Pacific Islands are the most aid-dependent region in the world. Foreign-owned multinational companies extract timber, minerals, oil, fish, and other natural resources. Economic dependence has forced many island governments to promote large-scale development, rapidly expand tourism, and accede to the military ambitions of past and present colonial powers. p. 32.

12.   The infamous security clearance program, the most important of the economic constraints imposed by the U.S. Naval government to secure U.S. sovereignty in Guahan, was not lifted until 1962. In his essay "The Economic Development of Guam," economist Anthony Leon Guerrero puts it rightly: "The security clearance was intended to maintain the military security in Guam...After 1950, the civilian government continued to justify the security clearance requirement as a way to protect the people of Guam from exploitation from outsiders. Of course, the fact that the people of Guam were already being exploited by the federal government was disregarded." p. 92.

the truth of our relationship and it is that there really isn't one. Deliberately retarding our chance of becoming self-sufficient, the U.S. turned our island into one big military installation run by the Navy. Under the dictatorial leadership of a single naval commander, who embodied the executive, legislative, and judicial branch of our government, many of us perished – died in service to our colonizer's military (which was largely held as our way out of a struggling post WWII, post-mass land condemnation Guahan) and died to ourselves. Or left. That is why there are more Chamorus in California now than there are here at home.

That is also why we are not surprised that our colonizer is hurling mockery at the U.N. Why should such statesmanship on the part of the U.S. surprise anyone anymore? The U.N., the reed forced to bend in the wind of too great a cost – moral and humane – is the very organization the U.S. failed, at least ideologically, at its very outset. And this should no doubt be counted by humanity as one of the gravest offenses of the last century, the most squandered of opportunities for peace lost on the shoulders of men.[15]

While these facts remain, so too do a mountain of questions we are growing less and less inclined to ask. Questions about why we are over-represented in the local prison and the various branches of the U.S. armed forces. Why we keep sending our boys and girls to fight for a country currently run largely by men obsessed with war, prodded on and on by a seemingly insatiable greed? A country whose president we

---

13.   This is a well understood point among the global community of colonized people. In the article Colonial Immigration in Guam in *Kinalamten Pulitikåt: Siñenten I Chamorro: Issues in Guam's Political Development: The Chamorro Perspective*, Leland Bettis writes: "It has always been understood in international circles that colonial powers should not allow immigration into the non-self-governing territories under their control. The reason for this is simple – if immigrants are allowed into non-self-governing territories, they may eventually outnumber and supplant the native people, especially if they too expect and demand entitlements which rightfully belong only to the colonized natives." p. 111.

14.   For a wider understanding of Oceanic realities in regard to indigenous populations, the following excerpt from *Cultural Survival Quarterly: State of the Peoples* illuminates an important point: "Only in Australia, Guam, Hawaii, New Caledonia, and New Zealand are indigenous Islanders minorities in their own homelands," as quoted in Oceania: Islands, Land, People by White and Lindstrom, p. 32.

cannot vote for, whose Congress has the authority to crush any attempt of ours to right our colonial condition, a Congress that has already wiped clean the sweat of our most brave and honorable legislative labor. All this stored away like a warehouse of unspoken, nay still un-thought, cardboard boxes of blocked social theory and action. Such is how Chamoru imaginations have been robbed of their critical functions. Such is how 'decolonization' came to be the tentative word on the tip of too many a tongue.

An Indian friend recently asked what, if anything, can the outside world witness in the example of Guahan? I remember thinking of the way it looks when the first light of morning struggles to the surface, when a well-rested sun wrestles itself to wake and rises, even if reluctantly, on the horizon. I told her with a kind of gravity, yes, that this was it. That though we are a disfigured people we are not a decimated one. That inside the heart of the Chamoru is an ocean of latent potentialities waiting to surge. Like morning, we are struggling to the surface. And we will break it. And when we do, it will be a beautiful day indeed.

Five months ago I read in the paper that a Chamoru photojournalist has again won international acclaim. In 1989, one of our own won journalism's top award, the Pulitzer Prize, for his feature photography. He received another prestigious award this year – the Robert F. Kennedy Journalism Award for International Photography, for his series on the Hmong migration to the U.S. The RFK award's distinguishing mark is that it recognizes journalists who use their work to elevate a disenfranchised community. In this case, the Chamoru photographer covered the Hmong refugees in exile from their homeland Laos.

---

15.   Use of the word "men" here is purposeful, as it is worth noting that both international politics and the military are so largely male-dominated spheres of power. It appears obvious that the promised peace of a post-WWII world was in fact lost largely on the shoulders of men. "Men" is not used generically, as to be inclusive of both sexes; in no way does it suggest a subscription to the false notion of gender-neutrality, especially considering how that neutrality is often nothing more than a cruel covering of all those varied silences choking oppressed women – who, as Audre Lorde says, are always the ones being forced to bridge the gap between blindness and humanity.

I sat quietly, paper in lap. I thought: here we have this talented Chamoru artist winning this award for his photographs of the Hmong people when his own people are oceans past disenfranchisement. Then clarity came like a breeze through the heart. The photographs the Hmong experience afforded him bespeak a larger national and global phenomenon – the obsessed nature of crises reportage, the drama of seeable suffering. The oppressed of the world is writhing on the covers of enough newspapers and magazines, the tragedies of the third world usurped by the gluttony of the first, fascinated.

The consciousness of the Chamoru – a people so long lacerated by colonial lashes that we have little blood left to bleed – cannot be photographed. To survive we must reach farther inside our mutilated minds than we have yet to do, beg an honesty we have not yet forced ourselves to face, and pull out from this place whatever small hopes have survived there. Only from there can we find things of any use to us. To combat the forces of our colonization, which is ever centering on our own internalized colonial thinking, we have no other option. What of all the wars being waged on the indigenous world, which never quite makes the magazines? What of wars which cannot be seen, but only felt, in the deep interiors of long colonized folks trying desperately to move against militarization, corporatization, and a worldview so spitefully oppositional to theirs and winning? What of us?

In the end, our victory is most a matter of how badly we want to survive.

Survivors: Ready your arms.

Lament of a Lost Chief

More than half a century after the rule of international law first wetted the lips of the world's statesmen with its sweetness, the Chamoru people of Guahan have yet to taste the fruit of that law. Denied our inalienable right to exercise Self Determination, decolonization for us remains a desolate dream.[16] With the creation of the United Nations at the turn of the last century, Self Determination carried with it a promise of justice so lamentably overdue for the colonized of the world. Because the organization's charter held the principle inviolable, it is clear that the government of the U.S. understood this international obligation as a signatory to that charter. When the U.S. placed Guahan on the list of the world's Non-Self-Governing Territories (NSGTs) in 1946, it pledged to aid us in the process of transferring power back into our hands. Side by side with other colonizing States, it participated in the creation of principles that promised to guide humanity into a new day.

Here, however, we understand that our administering power has betrayed and continues to mislead the international community. In other words, we know just how long the day has been. We know that much of it is already gone and a myriad hopes and, by consequence, a myriad lives remain deferred. It is worth noting from the outset that many informed people believe that the million-dollar question regarding Guahan and her people is contained in this single principle of international law: Self Determination. After all, because of this law folks living in eighty former colonies (nearly 750 million colonized human beings) have had their shackles – at least formally – removed.[17] Coming

---

16.   For more information about how the Chamoru people have been denied our right to exercise Self Determination, one should see the video: "Let Freedom Ring: The Chamorro Search for Sovereignty." For explicit proof of the legal mandate of the U.S. to aid the Chamoru people of Guahan in the process of Self Determination, consult Article IX of the 1898 Treaty of Paris, Chapter XI, Article 73 of the U.N. Charter, and U.N. General Assembly Resolutions 1514 and 1541. Further, one should read *Chamorro Self Determination: The Right of a People, I Derechon I Taotao.* I use the language "desolate dream" intentionally, to highlight the fact that even though the Chamoru case for Self Determination is sound it is denied to us by those in power who have an interest in preserving the status quo.

off the heels of World War II, the human race – for the first time as an organic unit – felt the stirrings of a higher station. The borders of the possible pushed back by human will, a new race of men and women set out fashioning a global polity it hoped carried the seed of a more just, more *civilized* civilization.

Meanwhile, a people thousands of miles of ocean apart, remained apart.

The Chamoru people have yet to come in from the cold. And our case for decolonization is sound from every legal and moral standpoint. Arguments honed throughout the last five decades have fallen vainly on the deaf ears of impotent statesmen; they continue to go unanswered one contemptible decade after another.[18] Beyond the U.N. Charter, we have since added U.N. Resolutions 1514 and 1541, of 1960, to the stockpile of legal ammunition used against our colonizer. The first of these cemented Self Determination as a "right" of all colonized peoples, no longer merely a principle. The second listed the three ways in which a NSGT could attain a full measure of self-government – free association with an independent State; integration with an independent State on the basis of complete equality; or Independence.[19] The following year, 1961, witnessed the creation of the Special Committee on Decolonization, or the Committee of 24, formed to appeal to administering powers to take necessary steps to decolonize those places still on the list of NSGTs. Its member states are themselves former colonies who meet annually; we have long since brought our case before them, to no avail.[20] Added to this is the other fact that the U.S. is in violation of its own domestic law, specifically Article VI, Clause 2 of the U.S. Constitution, which recognizes international treaties as the "supreme law of the land" and binds the federal government to them.

Chamorus vested in the struggle to protect our rights are left only to conclude that our case for Self Determination, one so utterly

---

17.   For more information, one can consult the official online site of the United Nations at < www.un.org >. As a point of clarification, it is important to recognize that while the planet's former colonies may have formally exercised Self Determination, so many of them are still cruelly constrained by the ill intrigues of international politics, which, under the guise of free trade and development, has not actually allowed or helped these fledgling States and their flailing economies to grow.

legitimate and long-standing, is simply not enough to effect change. Since the first of our political pushes to right this wrong, we realized that though we have the rule of international law on our side, this law is apparently not authoritative. At least not enough. The question must be begged then: what good is international law if it is so callously disregarded by the world's most powerful nation? How gripping can it be when our international institutions are dominated by the more powerful States? As our colonizer continues cleverly maneuvering its way around our concerns, it is busy disregarding the concerns of the international community in another underhanded operation – its 'War on Terror.' Like a youth too arrogant to believe there is any need of outside input or too stubborn to listen when such input is offered, the U.S. continues hurling stones of mockery at the U.N. – the very institution that is the bastion of human potentialities in the infant years of this century. Assailing the dignity of the collective to chase its insatiable

---

18.   The field of scholarship and work often referred to as Chamoru activism stretches back to no exact date. Arguably, it began as early as those first conscientious Chamorus recognized the U.S. violation of the 1898 Treaty of Paris. In the pre-WWII period, expressions of Chamoru resistance took the form of petitions to the federal government and were made repeatedly – in 1901, 1917, 1925, 1929, 1933, 1936, 1947, 1949, and 1950, according to Scholar Anne Perez Hattori, who also holds that these efforts were "consistently thwarted by U.S. naval opposition to citizenship and civil rights for the Chamorro people." Hattori asserts that it was this consistent opposition to Chamoru rights by the federal government as well as a growing discontent with the impotence of U.S. statesmanship among Chamorus that eventually led to the climactically important Guam Congress Walkout of 1949 – which led to the signing of the Organic Act the next year. In addition, Chamorus embarked on a dogged, decades-long struggle for federal recognition of their rights in the post WWII period, resulting in, to name a few major events: two Constitutional Conventions pushed forward by an active legislature in the 70s; a plebiscite on political status options in 1982 that led to a draft Commonwealth Act in 1987, which died after more than ten years of unsuccessful discussion with an uncooperative federal government; the gaining of organizational posture in the eighties with the creation of Chamoru activist groups, etc. The above quotation can be found in Hattori's essay, published in *Kinalamten Pulitikåt: Siñenten I Chamorro: Issues in Guam's Political Development: The Chamorro Perspective.* p. 58.

19.   For more information, see the official online site of the United Nations at < www.un.org >.

20.   Ibid.

greed into the corners of the world, Uncle Sam is largely responsible for the new waning of an old promise.

But perhaps the best beginning to this Self Determination story is the simplest one – fact versus falsehood:

The lies, in brief, are as follows. The U.S. is not illegally occupying this island; the Chamoru people are incapable of self-government; we have all bought what we've been sold; we are incapable of thinking, at least critically.

The facts, at first glance, are likewise uncomplicated. The most basic one is as follows. The U.S. is in violation of international law as well as its own Constitution in regard to its scheming statesmanship with its little piece of paradise so close to the Asiatic world.

Despite being perceived as simple-minded folk by those poisoned with internalized colonial thought, none of us, it must be said, are so simple-minded as to count our suffering the worst American imperialism has exacted on the planet or in the Pacific for that matter. But we do hold that of the U.S' other secrets, we may be its best-kept one.

Added to ample locally-led initiatives to realize self government in the pre WWII era, when for more than forty years we lived under successive U.S. Naval dictators incapable of governing our distinct sociocultural homeland, we've made even more initiatives in the post-war period.[21] All have crumbled in the face of Federal-Territorial relations.

What we do have is something called the Organic Act of 1950 – that alleged liberty. Stemming from the U.S. Congress and not from any act of Chamoru sovereignty or true consideration on our end, it was initially seen as a great step forward in the advancement of our rights, granting us such things as U.S. citizenship and a framework for a civilian government. It may have been a step forward but more than fifty years is a long time to wait for a second step; yet this is precisely what we're expected to do. Wait. And assume the tired position of the docile Chamoru. Today, as the forces of global hegemony deepen human misery throughout the already sore harassed indigenous world, this is a shamefully inadequate option. The Act, which is in no way an indication

21.   Arguably, anyone who would hold that a single U.S. Naval governor in a tyrannical post could possibly be capable of ruling our people for forty years in a post-WWII Guahan is in the least gravely ignorant and in the worst vulgarly racist.

that we have exercised our right to Self Determination, is a text whose time has passed.

Following the passage of the Organic Act, twenty years would pass before we could vote for our own local governor; the first elected (non-naval, non-appointed) governor took office in 1971. It wasn't until the following year that we were allowed one delegate to the U.S. House of Representative – one non-voting delegate to be accurate. Today, more than thirty years later, our representative is still without a floor vote. And Senatorial representation for our island is non-existent. So in Guahan the word 'vote' falls to the soul like it does in a Pablo Neruda poem – listless.[22] We remain unable to vote in federal elections in spite of the fact that we stay fixed to federal laws, restrained by federal regulations, caught in the straight jacket of the federal desire to cement its military presence in our home.

It must be noted here that every effort made to realize the decolonization of this island has been locally initiated. We acted and the U.S. reacted. And what the U.S. has been active in can only be counted as counter-action, or action intended to push Chamoru Self Determination into a blurred and endless horizon. Particularly, from four successive sessions of our legislature – the 12th to the 15th – we have fine examples of statesmanship. We have leaders who sharpened our case in the halls of *Hagåtña* (our paramount village) and brought it to the U.S. elite in Washington and to U.N. members in New York. U.S. statesmen did not give us their ears. Instead, in 1976, they gave us yet another Act of Congress –the Enabling Act. This one, no better than its predecessor, provided for the creation of our own constitution. Alongside the Virgin Islands (another of its territories), we were "allowed" to fashion a constitution for ourselves but under the condition that U.S. sovereignty remained a part of it.[23] Like tailors with

---

22.   Neruda, in his book *Twenty Love Poems and a Song of Despair*, uses the word listless often to describe the face of his beloved. Of love and lethargy he has written much. In the author's appropriation of Neruda's work, what is ascertained about this kind of raw love is that with it comes exhaustion. This is how Guahan in the first essay: "listless like a woman grieving her lost beloved." Guahan as like a woman who intimately knows such Nerudian love. She holds her people lovingly, even if so many of us are lost and entangled in the trappings of the pettier argument. Because so many of us are not yet passing into sight, her love of us is killing her, exhausting her unforgivably.

discriminating taste, we knew nothing of worth could ever be "fashioned" from such fraudulent fabric.

Today we can only regard this as terribly ironic. The same country that has its ideological roots in revolution – the urgency for freedom from the oppressive Britain, which caused it to suffer taxation without representation – is now, and has been for the last half century, exacting here the most extreme kind of taxation without representation thinkable.[24] Apparently, we are not worthy of voice in Washington. What we are good enough for is to fight and die for the U.S. on foreign fields. In fact, if the outside world only knew that, given our size, we have suffered the highest number of fatalities per capita serving our colonizer during World War II, the Korean War, and the Vietnam War, I trust that the heart of the international community would soften and gradually find the words to some song of solidarity.[25] *If we could find some stillness sanctified above the noise that is the matrix of militaristic patriarchy crippling our critical thought, I trust even more that some small window of liberation would open, that we ourselves would open up to ourselves.*

Of war there is grievous much to say. In the last world war, a key part of the U.S. military's invasive actions included a policy of land grabbing on the grandest scale. By the end of it, the U.S. had illegally taken control of 2/3 of our total real estate under the all-too-familiar guise of national security.[26] But this was just a pretext to unjust land seizure; in fact, the U.S. also took land away from native people for the recreational use of military dependents and displaced hundreds of people in the process.[27] This was part of a larger plan to use our island as the base for U.S. strategic posturing (insert muscle-flexing) toward Asia. And so we have it: Militarization. Nuclearization. Radical

---

23.   Souder-Jaffery, Laura (1987). A Not So Perfect Union: Federal–Territorial Relations Between the United States and Guam in *Chamorro Self-Determination: The Right of a People, I Derechon I Taotao.* Micronesian Area Research Center, University of Guam. p. 24.

24.   Laffer, Arthur B. (1980) Imperialism Alive on Guam, *The Sunday News*, n.p., as quoted in Souder-Jaffery, Laura (1987). A Not So Perfect Union: Federal–Territorial Relations Between the United States and Guam in *Chamorro Self-Determination: The Right of a People, I Derechon I Taotao.* Micronesian Area Research Center, University of Guam.

25.   Ibid.

Dispossession. The legacy of the American imperialist project in Micronesia.

What is often overlooked in property discourse, however, is the concept of eminent domain, which does not apply to the illegal taking of our land by the U.S. Under U.S. law, eminent domain is the legal appropriation of private property by the State without the owner's consent. The intent of the law is that it only applies to citizens of the State. Being a colonized people and not yet citizens when U.S. land seizure reached its peak means that this massive land grabbing is not only absurd in regard to its obligations under international law, but also illegal under U.S. law. U.S. law ensures that eminent domain is tempered by the State's obligation to provide just compensation for such takings. Here, 'just compensation' exists only in the empty imaginings of people who have yet to be seasoned by the realities of historical record. Such record is sullied by centuries of indigenous blood and hopes already spilled in the name of waiting on Justice.

Instead of just compensation, what we did see was another sly attempt by the U.S. to keep our land out of our hands. In 2002 the U.S. Fish and Wildlife Service tried to establish a critical habitat for local wildlife here; they designed a plan to use 24,800 acres at the northern end of our island for this habitat.[28] Our colonizer seems to counts the animals of Guahan more important and deserving of land, of a home, than the people of Guahan. Such is the nature of an Unincorporated Territory and her people – not counted, but discounted. Not persons, but property.

26.　　Bettis (2002), Ibid. Another important point to note here is how the U.S. tried to seize land under the "guise" of national security, which was in reality a pathetic pretext to a crude project of unjust land appropriation. In the article Righting Civil Wrongs: Guam Congress Walkout of 1949, which won the 1993 Janet Bell Pacific Research award, Pacific Islands Scholar Anne Perez Hattori Perez writes: "By 1948, the naval administration was condemning lands almost exclusively for the recreational use of military dependents. In Agana, roughly 500 people were displaced when 82 lots were condemned for a park and in Tamuning, 60 hectares of Tumon Beach were condemned for a military recreational center. Chamorros were further perturbed to see fertile lands seized by the military sitting idle." The above quote can be found also in *Kinalamten Pulitikåt: Siñenten I Chamorro: Issues in Guam's Political Development: The Chamorro Perspective.* p. 60

27.　　Ibid.

28.　　Critical Habitat Proposed. (2002, October 17). *Pacific Daily News.*

Another war the U.S. has waged on Chamorus is one it waged more directly on our neighbors in the Marshall Islands. Almost immediately after WWII, the U.S. decided to use our Micronesian kin as human guinea pigs in its secretive nuclear testing. In Enewetak alone, the U.S. dropped 66 atomic and hydrogen bombs between 1946 and 1958.[29] During Operation Bravo, the single largest nuclear "experiment" conducted in history by the U.S. government and the most infamous of these crimes against humanity, a bomb one thousand times the power of that which destroyed the Japanese city of Hiroshima in WWII was dropped on tiny Micronesian atolls. This is the story of U.S. administration over its 'Trust Territory.'[30] Before this, the U.S. launched the Enola Gay from the land of the Chamoru people, which dropped the bombs that ripped through Japan, thereby ushering in the nuclear age.[31] As our Marshallese kin continue today to suffer from astronomically high cases of cancer, tumors, and miscarriages, we here – 1200 miles west of Enewetak – were not spared the legacy of these nuclear transgressions.

U.S. military planes flown through the plumes above Enewetak to measure radiation levels were routed to Guahan (its convenient service station) for cleaning. U.S. Naval vessels contaminated with radioactive fallout were brought to Apra Harbor and nearby Cocos Island for decontamination.[32] For the last fifty years, the U.S. military has tried to evade accountability for this lethal contamination. While acknowledging wrongdoings in its Trust Territory and in some cases paying due reparations, it has for too long denied us similar recognition.

---

29.   Salvador, Richard in The Nuclear History of Micronesia and the Pacific. (1999, August). This article can be accessed online at < www.wagingpeace.org/ articles/1999/08/00_salvador_micronesia.htm >.

30.   The U.S. is not the only colonizing State with a history of nuclear weapons testing in the Pacific. In the above-cited article, Richard Salvador writes: "In French-Occupied Polynesia, 180 tests were conducted for over 30 years beginning with atmospheric testing in the Tuamotos in 1966. Only sometime later did the testings move underground in the atolls of Moruroa and Fangataufa...Tahitians and Marshall Islanders who were exposed, including test site workers, have been dying slow, excruciating deaths. Often they are unable to receive proper medical treatment because French authorities continue to deny officially that the nuclear tests did in fact cause any significant environmental or human damage."

31.   Ibid.

Instead, their vulgar reports only claim that they didn't know what the long-term effects of this exposure was, or to what extent we in Guahan were affected.[33] As a matter of fact, in response to a letter dated December 2, 2003 from our congressional representative to U.S. Department of Energy Secretary Spencer Abraham, requesting documents pertaining to possible radiation exposure and contamination in Guahan from U.S. testing in the Marshall Islands during the atmospheric nuclear testing in the Pacific, Secretary Abraham responded by writing: "the Department of Energy does not have information about the release of radioactive materials into Guam waters from decontaminating Navy ships. That information is under the aegis of the Department of Defense."[34] Thanks to the uphill efforts and persistent pressure placed on our sluggish politicians by a small group of local people, the Pacific Area Radiation Survivors (PARS), such lies have been pushed into plain view. It is now public knowledge that we were directly affected by these harrowing acts of U.S. aggression.[35] As a result of their work, our congresswoman finally acted on this matter and has submitted a bill to Congress for consideration. The bill would place Guahan on the official list of "down-winders" to be compensated for radiation exposure. We are awaiting congressional action on this matter.

---

32.   The Blue Ribbon Panel Committee Action Report On Radioactive Contamination in Guam Between 1946-1958, Nov. 12, 2002 from the offices of Senator Angel L.G. Santos & Senator Mark Forbes, (Authored by Charles L.S. Briscoe, Edited by William M. Castro and Consulted by Robert N. Celestial). See also The Human Radiation Experiments (Final Report of the President's Advisory Committee) at < http://tis.eh.doe.gov/ohre/roadmap/achre/ >.

33.   Ibid.

34.   Secretary of Energy Spencer Abraham, in a response letter dated January 20, 2004 to Delegate Madeleine Z. Bordallo.

35.   Assessment of the Scientific Information for the Radiation Exposure Screening and Education Program of *The National Research Council of the National Academies of Science*, Washington D.C., pg. 183, "Conclusions: As a result of its analysis, the committee concludes that Guam did receive measurable fallout from atmospheric testing of nuclear weapons in the Pacific. Residents of Guam during that period should be eligible for compensation under RECA in a way similar to that of persons considered to be downwinders." The study was supported by contract DHHS 232-02-004 between the *National Academy of Sciences and the Health Resources and Services Administration*.

And the litany, inevitably, goes on. But the U.S. tactic here is not even original. It's the old game of delectable distraction. Distract the people with an unyielding adherence to ambiguity. Use lots of words and say nothing. The U.S. has grown quite comfortable claiming that it is actually vested in the business of encouraging political development among our people. To date it still toots this erroneous tune. Thankfully, the U.S. has not succeeded in tricking all of us. We know better. Some of us have not been tricked into forgetting the existence of more than 400 federal statutes that in one way or another control (insert cripple) our political economy.[36] We have not forgotten the Jones Act, which prohibits the use of foreign built boats operating here, or the USDA regulations that hinder our island's economic growth, shutting us out from nearby Asian agricultural markets – both of which perpetuate American domination of our economy.[37]

These things combined only agitate our anguish. It can be argued, then, that the best used weapon in the arsenal of U.S. federal-territorial policy is Despair. The purposeful creation of pervasive hopelessness. Cut off our legs so we cannot walk in a direction of our design and instead stay stagnant, made to beg for handouts. Knowing this, it comes as no surprise that many scholars consider our region nothing more than a welfare state reared by the hand of U.S. imperialism.

Thankfully, these things combined have not proven enough to destroy us. Disfigure but not destroy. Even though our political journey has been entirely uphill, we have won some specific battles. Despite combating the internalized colonialism crippling the majority of Chamoru minds and consequently our progress, Chamorus committed to a human rights agenda managed to wield a position of honor and acumen. The Organization of People for Indigenous Rights (OPIR), People's Alliance for Responsive and Dignified Alternatives (PARA-PADA), and now, *I Nasion Chamoru*, have all, to varying extents, paved the way a coming generation still needs to further. They have fought – and won – some tangible things. Since the seventies, leaders came

---

36.   Souder-Jaffery (1987)

37.   Guam Growth Council, Administrative Relief Program for Guam's Economic Development Constraints, February 20, 1979, pp. 1-39, as quoted in Souder (1987).

forward talking of WWII reparations, land return to original owners, a legitimate plebiscite, a draft Commonwealth Act, and a host of other issues all tied to the million-dollar Self Determination question. Our victories include the federal return of some real estate to original landowners, a move ignited by a series of grassroots protests in *Hagåtña* in the early 1990s.[38] The movement, led by *I Nasion Chamoru,* resulted in 8,000 acres of illegally held land given back to our local government. Local activists fought to have them returned to Chamorus and succeeded; our Ancestral Lands Commission is currently in the process of seeing them justly returned. According to the Commission, to date two hundred lots have been given back and 8,000 thankful families have been reunited with their land. And as a younger generation learns to look back more carefully, we are finding quite a list of those who have pulled their weight in this struggle – Angel Santos, Ed Benavente, Hope Cristobal, Jill Benavente, Laura Souder-Jaffery, Robert Underwood, Frank Lujan, Paul Bordallo, Antonio Won Pat, Rita Franquez, Ron Teehan, Chris Perez Howard, Bernadita Dungca, B.J. Cruz, Debbie Quinata, Richard Taitano, Katherine Aguon, Rufo Lujan, Al Lizama, Anna Marie Blas Arceo, Linda Teodosio, Carlos Taitano, Mike Phillips, Ron Rivera, and on. Like lovers of shells, we are walking a shore we did not know stretched so lovingly on, one studded with people who shone with splendor in the light of old resistance. These contributing members of our community have left markers along the way that offer true direction; and some of them today continue to walk at our side.

Given the nature of global relations today, however, in which the corporate project is undermining democratic principles everywhere and leaving human beings fewer and fewer options about how to arrange our lives, we, like our conceptualization of revolutionary politics, must evolve. What the older generation has left us is no longer enough. We must ask ourselves questions that force us to bend back the reeds of the new and the possible and be willing to engage one another in the honest exploration of what comes of that bending. What does it mean to be independent in an increasingly interdependent planet? What does it mean to be a sovereign nation when on almost every seeable horizon

---

38.   Again, it is worth noting that the struggle for human rights shouldered by Chamorus who have come into consciousness, has then and is now being waged in *Hagåtña*, our paramount village, where of late our government officials are pushing policy that is in a profound sense, anti-Chamoru.

national sovereignty is but a waning moon? If the U.S. and other proponents of unrestrained global capitalism are spreading neo-colonialist ideologies and policies throughout the world under the banner of trade liberalization, how different is the new colonialism from the old one? If the U.S. dominates the world's most powerful institutions – the international financial ones which include the WTO, the WB, and the International Monetary Fund (IMF) – what more do we need to be convinced that nationalism alone is no longer a banner to brandish, no longer a worthy or intellectually serious end, no longer a balm capable of bringing solace to our shattered lives?

The needs of humanity itself are evolving. There can be no room for nationalism in an era when our energies should be devoted toward the building of one planetary nation. Independence in an age of necessary interdependence is a concept no longer able to stand alone in the room of ideas the new century takes seriously. Notwithstanding the limitations of a nationalist paradigm or the newer realization that nationalism is not a flag the twenty first century recognizes, the Chamoru people still hold the right to Self Determination inalienable. Regardless. It must never fall under the paternalistic purview of the U.S. to permit. This stated, what I am most concerned about has something to do with the knowledge of how to grapple with the tension between conviction and openness, between moral indignation and humility, between the immediate knowledge of being right and the elevated knowledge that being right is not enough to bring about social change. This struggle became most clear in a public meeting about water privatization a couple of months ago in Senator Joanne Brown's office.

In a round table discussion, seated at the table of Voice, occupying the chairs of Importance, alongside relatively powerless members of our government, were the more powerful members of the Chamber of Commerce – one of the key players in the master plan to sell our island off piece by piece from under our noses. On the periphery sat members of the Chamoru community, including the former high-ranking woman of *I Nasion Chamoru* and employees of the local waterworks agency concerned with the potential loss of their livelihoods. In this meeting the people of Guahan, again, became the targets of articulate dismissal. Our voices were taken less seriously by our senator and our positions were dealt with as if they were uncultivated and unsophisticated, and were patronized as such. It turned out like so many other important meetings lately, in which the integrity of our ancient civilization and the people entrusted with its perpetuation are so deeply disrespected.

In Guahan there is a saying: when you free the land you free the people. But how do you free a people whose own are coming to be themselves the prison guards? We are hostages of the American imperialist project and have been for far too long, but what we are fast finding is that we ourselves - imbued with the poison of internalized colonialism – are now also holders of the keys to that prison. This is exactly how it felt to be among the outer circle that morning in Senator Brown's office – estranged in that spiteful space where water and oil are fated apart.

Amidst the recent clamor has come a call from the activist community. There is a growing sense among the community that we need a leader to pull us successfully out of this predicament. That we need an individual to rise to the occasion with charisma to champion our cause – be it to protect our water from being privatized; safeguard our government from being sold to the private sector chunk by chunk; stop the landfill from being built in Dandan, stop the senators, the governor, the Chamber of Commerce, and so on, from selling us down the river. In particular, there is a gripping nostalgia in our quarters, a longing for one leader in particular – the late Angel Santos. The range of this lament has grown quite sweepingly, in correspondence and late night conversations. Many of us remember him almost medicinally and regard him as a symbol of a lost chief, a man capable of guiding our people triumphantly into our future. One of our best beloved leaders, Anghet set the veins of our people afire in some ways that no one else did. His work and foresight were combined with a striking ability to electrify our people into awareness and action of our human rights. He commanded respect. His politics of empowerment, first as a grassroots activist then as a Senator, professed his deep and unrelenting love of us.

A man who hastened to hear with his own ears and see with his own eyes the deeper truths about revolution, the politics of social change, and the burning after justice and God, he quickened the languid hearts of the long hurt. The quality of light he shed on the assemblage of our tired, tethered hopes was arresting. Today, we appear unable to let his spirit go, rather we cling to him with increasing desperation as we navigate ourselves through the treachery of ill intent coloring our current political landscape. There are those of us who are waiting, yearning for another leader like him to rise from our ranks – to save the day. And then there are those of us who know this yearning is no longer something we can afford. How long must we wait for the coming of a recognition that the best and perhaps the only way to honor his memory is to continue doing the work, continue fighting with our words – words we discover by engaging one another, words we forge out of the limestone of our daily lives through which we wield a power beyond wordplay?

If we choose to sit around waiting for this One to come forth, then what good are our efforts? What good is the collective if the One is so obsessed over? Shall we wait until the evening of our lives to finally understand the truth, that we don't need any one individual in particular to save us, nay, to adhere to this would be but a confession of ignorance about how power works? Anghet was beautiful not only because he believed in us, but also – and far more importantly – because he built a life around that recognition. Each breath we take today to declare our love of him must, then, be burdened with the weight of an equal recognition if it is to be honest or worth his mention. We honor our dead by furthering their lifework. If we love him or desire to honor his memory, we must with moral precision arise to shoulder the weight of our own contribution to this struggle.

And the wisdom of Audre Lorde, that ferociously articulate freedom fighter in human history, falls devastatingly solemn on my heart: 'Without community there is no liberation.'[39]

At 23, I have the nerve to believe that we have everything we need. And we need what we always have. Each other. It is in this vein

---

39.   Lorde, Audre (1984). The Master's Tools Will Never Dismantle the Master's House, in *Sister Outsider: Essays and Speeches*. In this essay Lorde makes the distinction between fake community and authentic community: "Community must not mean a shedding of our differences, nor the pathetic pretense that differences do not exist." In it she goes on to declare: "...those of us who have been forged in the crucibles of difference...know that survival is not an academic skill. It is learning to stand alone, unpopular and sometimes reviled, and how to make common cause with those others identified as outside the structures in order to define and seek a world in which we can all flourish. It is learning how to take our differences and make them strengths. *For the Master's tools will never dismantle the Master's house.*" To gain an incomparably gripping understanding of the feminist expression "the personal is the political" one should read this literary, political masterpiece.

that another truth becomes clear. While we may be the aching shard of a promise the twentieth century did not keep, the fact that some of us still have the heart to believe in the power latent in human endeavor and that our home is still worth saving is…achingly beautiful. And that is something.

We have more lamentation than we can possibly use; it is time we let our chief go.

Peace be upon him.

Paddles in the Water

March 19, 2005
The late Angel L.G. Santos Latte Stone Park
Hagåtña, Guahan

I am honored to be here with you all. Today I would like to talk a little about the harms that lie in our way as we try to figure out how we, as a people, intend to survive through this scary and intimidating phenomena indigenous peoples the world over are experiencing – corporate globalization. Because of time, I would like today only to focus on one issue that has stirred up heated public conversation in the last few months – water privatization – and use it as a mirror on which to shine the light of the bigger picture of neo-imperialism.

Chamoru people: We are in a dangerous situation as of late. If we do not begin to pay better attention to what is going on around us, especially in regard to our elected and appointed officials' passionate attempt to privatize our most precious resource – water –then we soon will be even more ruined than we already are. One of the most threatening ideas on the conversation table is the local elite's push to privatize GWA, and a "push" is just what it is. What some of our leaders desire, in partnership with some very clever businessmen, is to take our water out of our hands, and put it in the hands of – yet again – wealthy people who do not have our best interest at heart, who do not have a stake here, who would just as easily see Guahan sink into the ocean, if we in fact were not so vital to the interests of American Empire. And that is a fact worthy of our deepest grief: that we, as an indigenous people, cannot afford to be so blindly trusting, even of our own.

Chamoru people: *We are an indigenous people.* But what does that even mean these days, especially to the young ones now? It means what it has since the start of colonialism – that we are a people who have a history we have been taught – viciously – to discount, to discredit, to overlook, and, finally, to throw out of a high window. We have a history that has been stolen from under our feet, or rather, our un-careful eye. And still, the

42

colonizers' hands are not the only ones stained. Ours are too. So many of us have bought what we have been sold. So many of us have forgotten, somehow, that we are a great people who have absolutely no reason to hang our heads. Or kneel. We have a history that is older and smarter and more stubborn and that stretches back four millennia – laughably longer than our history with colonization. We have a history filled with people who refused to simply lie down and die, but who chose to shine with the righteous light of indignation. We have Hurao – who told us with great love and great compassion: Let us not lose courage in the face of our misfortune. We are smarter than we think.

Chamoru people: You may be wondering what all this has to do with the issue at hand, privatizing our water. Everything, I am willful enough to believe. If we had a more solid grasp on who we are and what we have valued for so many years past, the question of privatizing our water would not even be up for debate. If we knew our history, really, I suspect we would start becoming whole again. We would give our shapeless outrage form, and give our indigenous understanding a home. And then allow ourselves three tears: one for our *maga'håga* (the first born daughter of the clan and our high chief and probably the one warrior among us who fought until the very last breath in her body); one for our children, to whom we owe a new and total re-direction of our lives; and one for ourselves, because we have been hurting too long, thinking we were not entitled to our rage, because every time we try to talk about reclaiming our very bruised pride as a people we have been wrongly called racist, and because too many of our brothers and sisters are still on their knees, believing (even if they are barely aware of it) that they are inferior to mainstream Americans, their money, and their worldview.

And if a fourth should come, welcome that too. It may be one of joy, simply, because though we may be dormant, we are not dead yet. And we are definitely not for sale.

In the past few months, I have been feeling more and more afraid to admit what I am coming to believe – that here in Guahan we have a local elite willing to sell off our island in chunks and unwilling to talk about what Senator B.J. Cruz

43

rightly called the elephant in the middle of the room, or social economics (money), and a still very, very substandard relationship with the U.S. Of the elite there is more to say and even more to be saddened about. In the end, I think the fact that fewer and fewer of our leaders are strong and morally-grounded enough to talk about that elephant is the more bitter of their betrayals, a bitter that lingers in the collective mouth. But what they don't know is that the elephant is not the only thing in that room: there is also a light, maybe even one from God, shining down into it as well. And those of us who still somehow manage to muster up the kind of deep love needed to keep going about the business of saving our lives – we know enough to take our cue from that light. We know that the men and women who call themselves our brothers and sisters, who parade around in positions of power and continue to come bearing only the gifts of cynicism, frustration, and hopelessness are not who they say they are, and that they can keep what they have brought. We have had enough of that.

And so there are those who make it their business to go about assaulting our intelligence and our dignity. But maybe, just maybe, that is a reality that will work in our favor, in the eleventh hour. Maybe the local elite and others who have no stake in our home save fiscal ones have so fully convinced themselves that we are such an unintelligible, small-minded, stumbling people that we will never be able to find our footing. But we know better. We know in the end that the principles of democracy are so often bragged about but so rarely ever actualized and that the same people who laud the noble ideals of democracy and declare that because we are tied to the U.S., we are so lucky to be counted in the small circle of those who got it "right," are the people who are so quick to crumble in the crossfire of thoughtful confrontation. And the business of confronting, I believe our present situation makes urgently obvious, should be the business of our daily lives. Should be where we go to town. We know that we are smart and capable and that we have survived many an oppression and many a paternalistic administrating power. And despite their best attempts, we are still here, and some of us have long memories.

Brothers, sisters, cousins, daughters, sons, husbands, wives, children, grandchildren. Lost ones, forgotten ones, ones waiting to be called to life, ones who have fallen, and ones who are bound to fall – at least from grace. It is you I'm talking to. The eleventh hour is not only real. It is here. Now is the time to get to work, coming up with countless ways to resist the perilous side of global hegemony and lend our weight to the global struggle to prevent any Power vying for accumulation of gross wealth and resource from taking not only our livelihoods but also what we live for – the kind of life we want, the quality of dream we dream, the aspiration that most moves our souls to action. Now is the time to demand accountability from our leaders. Their loyalty made visible. Their words put into action. It is also a time to pray. For the spiritual destiny of that scarred country, the U.S., and for ourselves, that we may come into a compassion real enough to enable us to do this unglamorous, long, painfully slow, revolutionary work of waking our people up. One by one.

Perhaps my uncle is right. He tells me that the spirit of the land is strong, and it is only the spirit of human will that is weak. If that be the case, Chamoru people, *Ekungok i sinangan-hu.* Listen to what I am saying. Guahan is still our island, our home, our destiny, our prayer. She is still fighting for us. The least we could do is pick ourselves up and fight alongside.

Si Yu'os Ma'ase. Thank you. God is merciful.

Today there are smarter bombs being dropped on us – bombs coming in the form of words that our leaders are crafting to confuse us. To mislead and maim us. The kind that cloud the connection between who we are and who we are being lured into becoming.

On the horizon of things vying for our most immediate attention in Guahan is a perilous agenda of mass privatization pushed by the local elite and our politicians who are fashioning of their policy new emperors with no clothes. Advancing like an army of people who will not be swayed, not even by the force of facts, they are launching one of the most underhanded kinds of political discourse and propagandizing our home has ever seen. Even though water privatization has proven to be a failed experiment across continents, they march on. Despite the fact that water privatization has failed disastrously over the last twenty years in country after country, including the Philippines, Bolivia, South Africa,

Argentina, and Indonesia, they press on as if deaf to the sound of the truth. But as the people in power in our various homelands are starting to gather, those of us engaged in resistance are proving equally resolute. We understand that access to water is a universal human right and that to privatize such essential infrastructure, especially under the hand of multinational corporations who are fast becoming water barons, is a clear and unabashed attempt to violate this inalienable right. We will not relinquish the last of the global commons to Market, at least not without a good fight. And this fight, we well understand, is not merely one over a natural resource but one over moral positions and worldviews.

At the time this goes to press, our island's power posse is pushing the privatization of our infrastructure and selling our flailing government piece by piece.[40] Most importantly, the elite appear bent on privatizing our water under a concession agreement model of privatization despite the fact that the concession agreement is the exact model tried – and failed – in all the fore-mentioned countries. They have designed their proposed concession agreement after the botched model used to privatize water in Manila, Philippines. There, after astronomical rate increases, one of the two private companies that won the bid for Manila's water systems, Maynilad, abandoned 6.5 million people when they backed out of a 25-year contract after just four years.[41] And, ours here is the largest attempt at water privatization currently underway on U.S. soil.[42]

Such facts have not proven enough to dissuade our leaders from this privatization path. Our public servants appear in a mad dash to sell

---

40.   Despite the dominant discourse that privatization is the best way toward GWA (Guam Waterworks Authority) efficiency, the discourse that demonizes our people relentlessly and negates our ability to manage our government, the government is "flailing" for a variety of sociopolitical reasons which are undoubtedly tied to the following issues: our status as an Unincorporated Territory; a political economy that has for years been strategically crippled by U.S. imperialist interests in our homeland; the very real disempowerment among Chamorus and other long colonized peoples who have internalized the poison of colonialism and have yet to experience liberation through a marriage of critical social theory and action; and an economy centered only on tourism and an increased military presence in Guahan, a reality which suggests that we have yet to come up with – or commit ourselves to – the building of an alternative, viable economy.

41.   Marsden (2003 February 3), p. 1 and See Logan, Marty (2003, February). Multinationals Ride Wave of Water Privatization, Investigation Finds. *OneWorld US.*

our home as fast as they can. In current proposals, the operation and management of our water and wastewater systems are to be outsourced to a private company.[43] Believing that we cannot run our systems efficiently and that the private sector will run a smoother operation, they are convinced that privatizing our water systems is in our best interest. Funny how the private sector is suddenly capable of safeguarding our "best interest." Funny how familiar this argument sounds. But this story really begins three years ago, in 2002, when the U.S. Environmental Protection Agency (EPA) filed a lawsuit against the Government of Guam and the Guam Waterworks Authority (GWA) for violating the federal Clean Water Act and Safe Drinking Water Act. In June 2003, the federal court issued a consent decree mandating GWA to fix their water and wastewater systems – amounting to $212 million worth of upgrades. According to the Consolidated Commission on Utilities (CCU), an agency created to assist our community in exploring ways to address the upgrades, that figure is now up to $220 million.

In their attempt to address the federal stipulated order, the CCU has demonstrated non-transparency, failing to adequately include the public in the initial stages of the process. In fact, it wasn't until after it had already taken a hard-lined pro-privatization stance that we were thought of at all. Skillfully sidestepping a public mandate to include the general community in the conversation, the four-person CCU team hired in April of last year a three-member consulting team to assess the matter of water privatization. The consortium, or the League of Three Big Boys, is made up of the following: The Black and Veatch Corporation, the U.S. based engineering, consulting, and construction company specializing in infrastructure development in the fields of water, energy,

---

42.	A common objection to keeping water in the public sector is that our government is the breeding ground for corruption and a widely held position is that a private company will be less corrupt and more efficient in managing water. The facts indicate that the opposite is true: Because a private company is not held to the same standard of transparency, it may spawn far greater corruption. This is added to the other fact that a private company does not have a stake in our community save a fiscal one, and thus profit (and not improving the quality of service) is its top priority.

43.	See the special report by Public Citizen's Water for All Campaign online at < www.wateractivist.org >. The local elite's agenda to privatize GWA is inexorably tied to a larger project of militarizing our island and this is why those of us engaged in anti-water privatization are not surprised that ours is currently the largest attempt at water privatization in the U.S.

and information that has developed 20 percent of water systems worldwide.[44] Next we have Hunton and Williams, the U.S. based law firm of 850+ attorneys well versed in privatization practices that have affected most of the world.[45] Last but not least is its only local arm, Duenas & Associates, Incorporated, one of the largest regional engineering consulting firms in business since 1979. To date, the people have yet to be truly –with any semblance of dignity or even political decorum – invited to this privatization party. Instead only the consortium, along with a select group of local elected officials, business leaders, and, of course, the U.S. military were asked to dine.[46] Knowing who came to dinner has afforded us a clear picture, which is why we are not surprised that privatization was so quickly brandished as our only option.

Aside from remaining deaf to the growing cries of our community concerned with protecting our water from the wallets of few, the CCU has taken a gravely irresponsible, and arguably, illegal course of action over the last two years. With no regard for the larger community, the CCU went out and hired this consortium and now the public – the very interest group it dismissed – is being forced to foot the bill. Of a doctor's visit we neither needed nor asked for. To date, the people of Guahan have already paid this consortium/League of Their Own $1.1 million dollars in consulting fees (the CCU decided to use ratepayers' money to fund this study). Merely "looking into" privatization has already put us further in the hole. Are we simply (insert limply) to wait and see just how far down this rabbit hole goes? Thanks, but no thanks.

Where there is oppression there is also resistance. Guahan's resistance to water privatization lies in the hands of a circle of young people who are most doggedly committed to saving their bruised home. A grassroots group called the Guahan Indigenous Collective, these foot soldiers are adding a sorely missed voice to the conversation. We are saying: we will not just roll over and play dead. Together we have learned much about social justice and struggle. We have determined that

---

44.   See Black and Veatch website at < www.bv.com >.
45.   See Hunton & Williams website at < www.hunton.com >.
46.   GWA Options Weighed. (2004, May 22). *Pacific Daily News*, Section: Local.

the word 'resistance' falls heavy in a place where the public space for real and open discourse is suffocating.

And so 'resistance' falls from the higher rungs of tired hopes. And we are tired. Our conversations with the older generation of indigenous rights activists have only made this reality even lonelier. Some of them are, quite frankly, exhausted. After all, they've been doing this for the last twenty years (protesting the federal government to return land to the Chamorus). Those others who aren't as tired have withdrawn even further because of cynicism. The plain, undecorated truth is that we are young Chamorus who have come into consciousness and are now trying desperately to convince our community to care. To give a damn. To persuade them that privatization matters, as does their absence from the conversation.

After attempting smaller efforts, the Collective sponsored a forum at the University of Guam hoping to penetrate the deceptive discourse on water privatization the local elite keeps peddling. Not naïve to the fact that we were (and are) up against some very key people in the local elite – the Chamber of Commerce, the CCU, some members of the legislature, the administration, the media, and more – we went ahead with the event. With an audience of about ninety people, we did what we could. We had invited one economist, one environmentalist, one former Senator and Speaker of the Legislature, and the Interim Manager of GWA. I was also chosen to speak from the perspective of a writer-activist.

Alongside such co-panelists, it was easy to feel tense at first about what my contribution should be, especially among such members of the community. Looking out at the audience before me, mostly young college students of whose ranks I only recently left, I breathed, then shared with them some of the preceding speech.

Are our leaders, who are embarking us on a project of mass privatization with closed and unflinching eyes, really that ignorant of the verities of the global political economy? Is our Governor in particular utterly unfamiliar with the experience of others who have followed that route; I am thinking now of the anything-but-shining examples of water privatization in South Africa, Bolivia, and Argentina.

In South Africa, the government cut off water to over 10 million people within the last two years alone because it could not afford to pay for the newly privatized service. And this despite a constitutional guarantee of access to water for all.[47]

In Bolivia, water privatization involving the U.S. based Bechtel firm led to the infamous "water war" of 2001 and to the price of water tripling after privatization. Now, before all the eyes of the world to see, Bechtel has the nerve to sue the government of Bolivia – the poorest country in South America – for millions of dollars under a bilateral investment treaty for losses in future profits.[48]

In Argentina, Suez terminated its World Bank (WB) backed contract to manage water and sewer services to Buenos Aires when the financial meltdown of the state's economy meant that the company would not be able to maintain its profit margins. For the people of Buenos Aires, water rates were not reduced by 27 percent like the company projected, but instead rose by 20 percent. And the other fact that 50 percent of employees lost their jobs only intensifies this crime.[49]

Adding insult to injury, the WB last year demonstrated that it has no intention of getting off this train of destruction. Instead it increased funding for water privatization projects from US$1.3 billion in 2003 to US$4 billion in 2004.[50]

Despite the blatancy of these case studies, some in our community may still not believe in the inefficacy of water privatization; some may even try to counter them with a desperate desire to count us in Guahan distinct from these countries because we are not "third world." We do not belong to the third world; we move among the unnumbered. There are others, faces turned endlessly toward the continental U.S., who would only take case studies seriously if they came from there. Enter Atlanta, Georgia.

In Atlanta, the management contract used to privatize water was terminated after four years of what was supposed to be a 20-year arrangement. United Water, the private company that won the contract there, attributes its failure largely to problems with system data despite

47.   Barlow, Maude and Clarke, Tony (2004, January). Water Privatization: The World Bank's Latest Market Fantasy. *Polaris Institute*.
48.   Ibid.
49.   Ibid.
50.   Ibid.

the fact that all the firms that bid for Atlanta's contract knew of this data deficiency prior to submitting their bids.[51]

Atlanta is merely one of the many cities coping with the aftermath of failed water privatization projects across the U.S. Joining Atlanta are: New Orleans, LA, Indianapolis, IN; Laredo, TX; Felton, CA; Jersey City, NJ; Buffalo, NY; Lexington, KY; Santa Paula, CA; East Cleveland, OH; Bridgeport, CN; Rockland, MA; Angleton, TX; Lynn, MA; Lee, MA; Milwaukee, WI; and Stockton, CA.[52]Atlanta is but one of many U.S. municipalities bearing the brunt of a botched privatization, one of eighteen others regretting water privatization.[53]

It seems that what we are running out of is not viable alternatives to privatization but the patience with which to understand the quality of our politicians' foresight.

Believe it or not, our government may not be the biggest fish to fry. In the sea of those assaulting the intelligence and dignity of the Chamoru people is an even bigger fish – our not-so-free press. On second thought, we do have a free press. Maybe too free a press. By that I mean a press so free it is not merely reporting news, but feeling free to almost fabricate news. Our dominant newspaper and a subsidiary of the American-based Gannett Corporation, the Pacific Daily News (PDN) has not only taken a clear position in the political debate, it has *opened fire* on those of us opposed to privatizing our water. In a column titled "Our View," the editorial staff at the PDN has finally dropped the pretense of objective reporting. The order of the day is not reportage but rabidity, and as far as the privatization agenda is concerned, the editorial staff at PDN is playing less and less the role of reporter and more and more the role of red herring.I would share these things with our Governor, but to date the Office of the Governor has yet to respond; months ago I called his office trying to get an appointment with him.

---

51.   Slattery, Kathleen (2003). What Went Wrong? Lessons from Cochabamba, Manila, Buenos Aires, and Atlanta as part of *Annual Privatization Report 2003*. See the website of the Reason Public Policy Institute, a public policy think tank promoting choice, competition, and a dynamic market economy as the foundation for human dignity and progress at < www.rppi.org/apr2003/whatwentwrong.html >.
52.   For more information about how water privatization has failed in all the listed U.S. cities, see the special report by Public Citizen's Water for All Campaign online at < www.wateractivist.org >. Guahan is included in this June 2005 report.
53.   Ibid.

They took my name and number. I have yet to hear back. I have voiced these concerns to CCU Chairman on more than one occasion; they keep falling in vain on the terrain of his intentions.

Perhaps the most memorable of the editorials in the "Our View" column can be found in the May 28, 2005 issue, entitled "Just Do It: Elected officials need to move forward with concession agreement." Here is a sample:

> What more will it take for elected officials to realize that in order for the island's water and wastewater infrastructure to be fixed, it must be taken out of the hands of government? It's been shown time and time again that GovGuam can't efficiently or effectively run the island's water and wastewater systems…What more will it take for elected officials, including CCU members, to take the right course and move forward with a concession agreement.[54]

What is eye-catching about its tone is its emotional undercurrent. What is ironic is that the opposition to water privatization is rarely painted as anything besides emotional and uninformed.

To clarify a point of contradiction about the extent to which Lee Webber is involved in the production of the editorial column, I need to highlight two PDN articles.

More than three years ago PDN editorial editor Duane George won 2nd place in the Best of Gannett Contest for Editorials. In a PDN story published in May of 2002, George said he could not take sole credit for the award:

> I have to share credit with Lee Webber, the PDN's publisher and my managing editor, Rindraty Celes Limtiaco. *We collaborate on a daily basis*, and they have been instrumental in developing my writing abilities and skills.[55] [emphasis mine].

In another PDN article earlier this year, in which legitimate concerns about the dangers of water privatization was again painted as

---

54.   See editorial Just Do It (2005, May 28). *Pacific Daily News*, p. 14.
55.   See story, George Among Best of Gannett (2002, May 12), *Pacific Daily News*, p. 2.

emotional and the result of unsubstantiated "fear," Mr. Webber is quoted as saying:

> I don't work in the newsroom. *I do have something to say about the editorial position of the paper, but not the day-to-day news operations.* That's the executive editor's responsibility, not mine... You have to differentiate between Rindraty Limtiaco, who is the executive director in charge of the newsroom, and me, who is in charge of the newspaper as a company, not the news.[56] [emphasis mine].

The stench of contradiction is sharp.

Needless to say, the editorial staff is a busy bunch. It takes effort to launch a public relations campaign out of a daily newspaper, but they have friends to share the load. Friends in high places. Perhaps the most dangerous of the company they keep is the local Chamber of Commerce, or more particularly, its most ardent arm, the Armed Forces Committee. The fact that there is such a committee should scare us all. The committee is headed by PDN President and Publisher, Mr. Lee Webber. In addition to being the Chairman of the Armed Forces Committee today, he was the Chamber's Immediate Past Chairman in 2004.[57]

One of five standing committees in the Chamber of Commerce, the Armed Forces Committee combines the following players: the Chamber of Commerce, the Commander U.S. Naval Forces Marianas/ USCINCPAC Representative, Thirteenth Air Force (PACAF), 36th Air Base Wing (PACAF), Guam National Guard, and the U.S. Coast Guard Marianas Section. Apparently, they reached a cornerstone of understanding, the first three of five official agreements being: to foster goodwill in support of the military presence in Guam; act as liaison to facilitate a positive relationship between Guam's civilian and military communities; enhance public awareness of the important economic and socio-cultural impact of the military in Guam.[58] Anyone even a bit sensitive of our substandard relationship with the U.S. should be

56.   See story, Activists Worry, Officials Dispel Privatization Fears (2005, June 14). *Pacific Daily News*, p. 3.
57.   Ibid.

outraged not only with this list of agreements but also with these undoubtedly dubious connections.

Somebody sound the alarms.

The tragically inevitable tie that binds these boys is militarization. The one thing all these players have in common is the desire to increase military presence here. A power point presentation prepared by the Guam and Saipan Chambers of Commerce earlier this year affirmed this. In it was an unequivocal push to privatize not only our water systems, but our sewer and power systems as well. Privatizing our water, then, is just part and parcel of what can be called: Operation Load the Bases.[59]

In a leaked report dated November 22, 2002, the Chamber of Commerce Committee on Outsourcing and Privatization revealed that other agencies being targeted include the Guam Memorial Hospital Authority, our only civilian hospital; the Port Authority of Guam; the Department of Public Works; the Guam Telephone and Power Authorities; the Department of Education; and the Department of Corrections. Select services under each of these agencies are destined to be touched by the Chamber's caress, and some have already been. This reality bespeaks another: the Chamber is gaining far too much ground in Guahan.

And the cacophony continues. The Chamber, masquerading as "a group of citizen's committed to protecting Guam's water rights," has not steered from its course of deliberately misleading the public. A leaked copy of their campaign strategy outlines a list of twenty-two topics for the PDN opinion column. For a while, these opinion pieces ran on a near-weekly basis.[60]

Framing privatization as an unstoppable process beyond our control, this privatization posse is suggesting that the issue is beyond our capacity for synthesis. In public addresses, our Governor has made it clear that he intends to pursue the privatization of GWA, either in part or in full.

58. To see this list, one can visit the official website of the Guam Chamber of Commerce website at < http://www.guamchamber.com.gu/ >.
59. An online link to this power point presentation can be found on the Guam Chamber of Commerce website.
60. Sabina Perez, personal communication throughout 2005.

In his 2005 State of the Island Address earlier this year, privatization proved the prized bull of his policy, which, conveniently, is the same bull prized beyond measure by the Chamber. We have never before witnessed such a top-down, no-holds-bar PR campaign such as this one.

In the work of confronting imperialism, it is growing clearer that we have a larger task at our door. Fact alone falls short. Maybe it always has. It seems we must find a way, as Chamorus, as citizens of humanity, to come into a force more powerful than a merely retaliatory one. If we are to "win" anything at all, we must hone our compassion with the sharpening stone of moral indignation, and not be content with the mere rightness of our position. By the sheer force of our morality, we must shame immorality into visibility. We must doggedly keep up a second struggle entirely, one in our interior lives. One in which we stay uncompromisingly committed to a nonviolent spirit of humility. The true jihad.[61] We must also find practical ways to help our people make those connections and help our families and friends understand not only the nature of our struggle but also why we must. Help them, for example, to understand the root – the military-industrial complex at the heart of the local political agenda.

Some words from our Governor help clear this up; they cast a light with which to see why the Chamoru people seem so unable to shake off this colonial sleep:

> Our efforts at cooperation have not stopped at the local level, we continue to work closely with the Department of Interior to heighten awareness and renew interests from U.S. and foreign investors into our island. We have worked closely with Congresswoman Madeleine Bordallo and the Guam Chamber of Commerce to get the message out in Washington D.C. that Guam is ready for more military presence. And the message has been heard. Our close relationship with the Bush-Cheney Administration and the

---

61.   Jihad in Arabic means exertion and struggle. In today's post 9/11, strongly anti-Muslim world, it is often a word bruised, misunderstood, and misappropriated. In Islamic theology, it has a dual meaning. While on one level it means "holy war," on another level (one more profound) it alludes to an interior war – a deeply intimate struggle to overcome self, and ultimately submit to God in self-effacement. Islam means submission; a Muslim is simply one who submits. If we are to become global citizens, we must look beyond the easier veils covering deeper realities and truths.

Republican Majority in Congress will reap benefits for all
our people.[62]

With such alliances stated, we are figuring out just what
it is we are up against. But we understand. Our Governor is but one of
many of our people for whom the veil of colonial favor has yet to fall.
As indigenous folk, we mourn only his consequent loss of vision.

And as always, another question comes. Another one
altogether. Why should one of the longest occupied territories on earth
be expected to do anything other than follow suit anyway? Why should
leaders of a colony such as ours be expected to blaze an alternative
agenda, when leaders the world over are being forced to succumb to the
forces of a larger political game? Grasping that game requires a lot of
work and even more synthesis of social and geopolitical concerns. In
regard to this, I can share what I have learned about how the game
works.

In the world of corporate globalization, policy is determined
almost entirely by economics. By this is not meant the historical
understanding of economics, how human communities have organized
their lives around the practicalities of the rule of exchange. What is
meant here is the kind of vulgar economic theory that has in the last 50
years become the altar at which today's global politicians pray. The
economic theory being bullied into the farthest corners of the globe by
the heads of transnational corporations who are finding ever-more clever
ways to subvert democracy. Bending the already slouched backs of our
international financial institutions (IFIs), mainly the World Bank (WB),
the World Trade Organization (WTO), and the International Monetary
Fund (IMF), they are egged on more than ever now by the crude
Washington Consensus, the ideology coined in 1989 by John Williamson
of the Institute of International Economy. This consensus comprises
principles of economic policy that emerged from the consultation of the
Washington-based institutions which include the congress and
government of the United States, the IMF, and the World Bank,

---

62. See Governor Felix Camacho's 2005 State of the Island Address online at
< http://www.kuam.com/govguam/camachomoylanadministration/
officeofthegovernor/spee/ches/stateoftheislandaddress-2005.aspx >.

---

including bankers, transnational executives, politicians and finance ministers."[63]

As we all by now know, such a think tank would never, could never, be creative enough to come up with something that actually works for the rest of the world. A 2003 report by a collaboration of investigative journalists documents how privatization has cut off millions of people from safe water supplies. Resulting, for example, in South Africa's worst ever cholera outbreak, which killed nearly 300 people and infected more than 250,000.[64] In China, water is being cut off to small-scale farmers in the North because it is "needed" in its urban centers and for factories making sneakers for U.S. Markets. In India, peasant farmers have been driven off the land.[65] India is on a fast track of development – along with privatization has come a recent obsession with the construction of big dams that have displaced more than thirty million people in the last fifty years.[66]

Today the WB continues to force poor countries to commodify their water resources and sell them to the best bidder. Lending about $20 billion to water supply projects in the last decade alone, it has demonstrated that it is the principle financier of water privatization.[67] In fact, "the majority of WB loans for water in the last five years have required the conversion of public systems to private as a condition for the transaction."[68] In the 12 years covered in the report, the WB insisted that privatization take place in about 1/3 of the total water supply projects figured into the $20 billion. During that same period, one of the world's largest multinational corporations, Vivendi Universal, reported that its water-related revenue more than doubled, from $5 billion to more than $12 billion.[69] Vivendi is only one of the world's water wolves, only one of the corporations based in Europe and the U.S. holding planetary water hostage.[70] These players have "extended their reach" nearly five-

---

63.   (2004, March 31) CBC broadcast. *The Fifth Estate: Dead in the Water, The World Bank: A Private-Sector Fix for a Public Water Crisis*

64.   Marsden (2003, February 3), p. 1and See Logan (2003, Feb.)

65.   Mann, Peter (2004). Water Wars: A Report from the World Social Forum.

66.   Roy, Arundhati (2001). *Power Politics*, p. 20.

67.   Barlow and Clarke (2004)

68.   Ibid.

69.   Ibid.

fold in the past dozen years as they pursue political revenues estimated as high as US$3 trillion.[71] Together, the top three corporations alone had annual revenues of almost $160 billion in 2001 and those revenues are growing at ten percent a year, thereby outpacing the economies of the very countries in which they operate.[72]

To gain any real understanding of our situation here in Guahan or in Micronesia for that matter, analysis of the WB alone is insufficient because corporate globalization by itself is not the source of our regional calamity. More accurately, it is the American imperialist project finding in the other a friend. A story of U.S. imperialist agenda playing nice and neat into the larger project of corporate globalization.

In the Western Pacific region to which we belong, the blueprint for U.S. neocolonialism that has been and is still being used to hold our fledgling homelands hostage is the depraved Solomon Report. The 1963 report resulted from a mission that former U.S. President John F. Kennedy sent to Micronesia, with the known end being the ironing out of a policy to deliberately debilitate our region. Intended to secure U.S. sovereignty over Micronesia, it perpetuates and ideologically legitimizes unthinkable acts of aggression on our region. The mission, headed by Harvard University Business School Professor Anthony Solomon, firmly established U.S. imperialism in the Western Pacific.[73] On the regional bed it laid out a colonial dress we would be forced to wear for the pleasure of our patriarchal, militaristic master. To think that this is the very region "entrusted" to the U.S. by the U.N. after Japan's World War II defeat is sickening. Micronesia, on the whole, continues to convulse under the nausea.

---

70.   It is important to recognize that it is Europe and the U.S. – the white, western colonial powers that keep proving via the oppressive mechanisms of global capitalism that there in fact is nothing so new about neo-colonialism. These States, by pouncing on the poor of the world in ever-more sophisticated movement, are not free of responsibility for the perils of the global political economy.

71.   Marsden (2003, February 3), p. 3, quoting a report by the Center for Public Integrity's International Consortium of Investigative Journalists.

72.   Barlow and Clarke (2004)

73.   Richard Salvador (1999, August). Also, for more information about the Solomon Report, visit the Richard F. Taitano Micronesian Area Research Center, University of Guam.

So it seems our Governor is right on track – smiling alongside the rest of those leading the people blindly into the corporatization of our world. Some of us have detected the obvious: talk, especially theirs, is cheap. What we are witnessing today is not the glittering ends of a formula poised to uplift the poor from impoverishment. Instead what we are seeing is a small portion of the human race poised to pounce on the poor of the planet.

Like in other communities actively resisting the sharp edges of neo-imperialism across the world, here a small army remains. An army at work in homes and at village mayor's offices wading against the top-down tide of privatization. The hardworking people of GWA have not yielded. They continue to make marked improvements in our water systems amidst the frenzy from on high. They are working dutifully, though daily demonized by the press, to meet compliance deadlines and make substantial improvements. Despite the dishonest agenda of the CCU and the Chamber, they are making notable progress. In fact, according to the latest peer review by the American Water Works Association and the Water Environment Federation, they have improved their ability to provide safe water, stabilize water pressure, identify and repair leaks, and increase operator certification, among other accomplishments.

Most interesting in the review is they found it worthy to note that despite support by the people to keep the water in public hands, the business community keeps pushing privatization.

Thankfully, we have in our midst a thread of hope, a truly concerned citizen who has risen in opposition to these politics being pushed at the detriment to the people. Her name is Sabina Flores Perez and late last year she came home to lend a hand and voice to our water war. Leaving behind a job as a researcher with the University of California, she boarded a plane with not much more than the moral power of an open heart and a basic understanding of how water privatization has generally failed worldwide.

Sabina, widely regarded as spokesperson of the local anti-water-privatization movement, has come home to do the unglamorous, painfully-slow, but real work of revolution. Before seeing a film on the failed concession model of privatization in Cochabamba, Bolivia and realizing that our leaders here are now discussing essentially the same experiment with our livelihoods, she never even considered herself an activist. But as with other beautiful, ordinary people who come into social justice work with their marked qualification being a sincerity of heart, she has come to us like a light. In the past year she has managed to catapult the issue to the forefront of our attention. From school to news studio, radio to rally, panel to public hearing, she reminds the rest of us that the greater point is not that our island and people convulse under colonization's cruel hand but rather that common people – people who let their moral outrage politicize their love, who stay in the conversation though it continues breaking their hearts, people who, in their thirst for justice, find God –become the miracle.

And it has not been easy. Contributing to our conversation has caused her a great deal of pain. Having lived away from the island for many years, she was instantly considered – especially by the elite who kept finding ways to dismiss her – as more or less irrelevant, not credible. After all, who did she think she was? Who was she to tell us how we should proceed? They did not have to listen to her because she was apparently not "rooted" enough in this place, not "vested" enough in this community. These are the nature of the thoughts, spoken and not, that were thrown at her when she tried to contribute. These are the things with which they sullied her good name and nature when she tried to inform them with facts, when she spoke out on behalf of her people. Their actions professed what they really believed: that there was no place for her, a clear and well-informed woman. The presence of one armed with truth is often unwelcome by those who benefit from the status quo, from the way things are. In fact, she told me that at one point they just did not know what to do with her and in a kind of panic asked her to leave a public meeting. Not surprising. Just pitifully uncreative. She has since successfully pushed our struggle to protect our water resource into the national and international light. Our struggle is now listed among other U.S. communities on the Public Citizen's Waves of Regret national campaign to combat risky privatizations. We have also garnered support by scores of countries, organizations, and individuals who have signed an international sign-on letter opposing water privatization in Guahan.

In Sabina, we see a paddle in the water. With faithful strokes, she is making a difference. But, alone, she cannot apply enough pressure on our leaders to gain both their hearing and their hearts, to remind them of the moral obligation to safeguard our human rights, to interrupt the status quo of perilous politics marring most of the world. We cannot expect her alone – nor should we – to keep paddling so hard, in a kind of desperation, to steer a vessel we are all in.

If we remain unwilling to pick our paddles up, put them in the water and join her, then we do not deserve her.

Paddles up.

Coming Home

I have come to believe that good art contains the ability to reawaken the souls of people to the possibilities of life. It quickens the heart and enables us to still have hope even without absolute certitude. I count my first meeting with good art the moment I found womanism, or feminism of color, the scholarship that saved my life by affirming an intimate and insistent need for wholeness in social justice struggle. Womanism, rich in word and sound and quilt and color, artfully honors the work and ways of knowing of women of color, out of whom the world of racist patriarchy has tried to make a mule. It involves the writing, singing, believing, daring, hoping, and challenging of these women, who know too well that the margins of society is an inadequate space in which to work, too cramped a corner in which to chisel more just dreams. Because women of color work and create despite such depraved conditions, their art indicts the heart of dominant society, becoming the pulse on which the world of varied oppressions puts its finger. Born in compassion painfully earned, such art possesses a potency that permits us to consistently choose hope over cynicism, to choose to see the world for not only what it is but for what it could be.

Its humanness, honesty, tenacity, and insistence on the survival *whole* of the people caused so interior a movement it compelled me into evolution. Womanism is worth noting only because it is the one thing that finally forced me to face a truth I had long been unready to – the knowledge that to contribute to humanity, I had to struggle with my own people and see that sometimes the most revolutionary thing one can do is go back home, which is just what I did – returned to Guahan to engage my kin in the conversation of how to go about the business of saving our lives.

Upon return, I found a small group who called their experiment with freedom *Guma' Pålu Li'e,'* The House of the Seeing Mast. 'The House' is a community of chanters who have redeemed the art of traditional chant, built from a reconstruction of *fino' håya* (literally, the language of the south, the original language of our people, *I Manmatao*). Sanctified above entertainment, these chants are actual roads being walked toward a communion with the ancients. This movement, this endeavor of faith – this art – is a way home. Allowing one who chants them to change anguish into armor and outrage into some thing of safeguarded power, these chants are manifestations of the highest art. They help us reclaim indigenous identity, a process so personal in its closeness and so political in its consequences.

These chants allude to our people's pre-history and span the range of welcoming in from the sea a master navigator and honoring a specific clan of fisher folk to communal gatherings of elders and our creation story. We receive from them the sustenance our colonized, starved souls so badly need. Reviving the ancient tongue affords us an access to our past long sought out. Some chants speak straight to our matrilineal past. In some, we specifically call on the spirits of our women, in particular, past chiefs. By inviting them, connection is made, guidance asked for. On the whole they help us lift the colonial veil hindering our fullness of sight and a vision of our truer selves. Such art enables a juxtaposition of 400 years of colonization with a 4,000-year span of indigenous understanding, unfolding our empowerment, our self-determination. In my own life this has been among the most profound experiences of self-discovery and reclamation and healing. We have found that when we call out to the spirits of our women something happens – something to suggest we do not go unheard. In the days of the ancients, we organized our lives along matrilineal lines and our highest chiefs were our *maga'håga*. Our women guided with wisdom that sustained, and they are still lovingly and resolutely here. Like a surge from some inward ocean, our ancestors are coming back to us.

In one chant, we call out:

Guaifi I kulo' manaina. Å'gang sa' mannannanga I taotao-måmi.

Blow the shell trumpet of our elders. Call because our people are waiting.

The full measure of how these words allow us to come alive we will not share with the outside world. *The day for usurping indigenous secrets has come to pass.* What I can share is a story of an afternoon when I had only first come home, an afternoon I will never forget.

It was a ribbon cutting ceremony for a new operations facility for the U.S. Air Force aerial combat unit on the northern military base. To get there I was stopped at the gate, sponsored on the base by a senator I was accompanying. Once inside and past a magnificent view of the entire northern coast, I arrived at the start of the program to hear our Governor make a speech. I had heard him speak before, but this occasion was unique; the audience was asked to rise to sing the anthem of the U.S. Air Force:

> Off we go into the wild blue yonder,
> Climbing high into the sun;
> Here they come zooming to meet our thunder,
> At 'em boys, Give 'er the gun! (Give 'er the gun now!)
> Down we dive, spouting our flame from under,
> Off with one helluva roar!
> We live in fame or go down in flame. Hey!
> Nothing'll stop the U.S. Air Force!

When it was over, we were asked to take our seats and our Governor proceeded to talk to us about the wonderful occasion we were there to applaud. I listened to our highest elected public servant do such a disservice to the Chamoru people. He went on about the construction of the facility honoring the Chamoru people because at its main entrance stood two latte stones, the latte being one of our most prized cultural symbols. He went on to assault the dignity of the Chamorus by saying things such as how nice it was that the architect thought to include the latte, how that day was a day to celebrate because the increased military presence on Guahan was welcomed proof of our economic growth and viability. After standing up, hand to heart, singing such a violent, militaristic and patriarchal song – on land being occupied by the U.S., land our people are not allowed to access, land once owned and passed down through the women's line – I felt embarrassed. For him at first and then for all of us.

A single year of being home after a four year sojourn has opened my eyes to many things – that the real war to be waged here is one for our people's attention; that 'war' is a word I have never before been so hesitant to use; that a word to be carefully considered and even more carefully used is 'art.'

Jawaharlal Nehru of India suggested once that art is the true mirror to the people's minds. Oppressed people have long come into an understanding of art as a power that gives voice to new possibilities. The oppressed own the knowledge that art has political and even revolutionary dimensions, if used in the service of our vision of freedom.

Here in Guahan – a colony silently convulsing under an unnamed pain – we desperately need a new definition of art. We must join our indigenous kin who have learned to wield art as weaponry in a world of destructive forces set against us, who have learned, at least, that real art is divorced from ego.

The overriding need of today is unity. From our diversity must come a force of connectedness. We must learn to pull in the strands of our varied endeavors and tie them to the primary project of simply surviving. The arts community is well aware of the 'crabs in a bucket' conversation; we have it enough to understand that this syndrome stifles growth of the seeds of empowerment and revolution latent in our art. As artists, maybe what we need first is to allow ourselves to sit with the pain of our separation, acknowledge it as real, and allow ourselves to move through these feelings.

What we do have is an invitation of our nobler selves to work together toward a common end, the building of a long-overdue cultural center. We are united in our understanding of the urgent need for such a center, a home to house our art, our artifacts, our edifices of endured culture. Increasingly made minorities in our own home, suffocating under the weight of too many neo-colonialist cloaks, a cultural center could catalyze from our varied endeavors a more fortified front. Together we own the knowledge that our art *can* ameliorate our condition, *can* breathe life into our people poisoned with internalized colonialism. This knowledge is enough to call us to connection.

In political circles, leaders are no longer leading and perilous, profit-driven agendas and solely economic concerns are crushing other social and cultural concerns. Sharp tongues are proving sharper than sharp people in much of our tired discourse. We are becoming too comfortable hurling insults and mockeries at one another, and disrespect is outpacing the desire to actually engage. It is a shameful state of affairs when we are so busy posturing that we are no longer poised to do anything real to elevate our station. *As a people we are allowing ourselves to remain divided, and by respectively small issues, when all the while our very annihilation looms on the nearest horizon.* This reality forces another: the art we most need is not – cannot – be contained any longer in its usual categories. Visual, literary, performing. And its purpose, those ends our art envision, must likewise be furthered.

We need to agonize the edges of these categories, push back the borders of what we've long accepted as the realm of what we can and cannot accomplish. If our art continues to remain separate from our spirituality and true indigenous heritage, we will likewise remain separate. If we do not learn to tie the remaining shards of our hopes to the truth that real art cannot exist without the humility of true spirituality, what we create can only fail to call us to life. And our mirrors will only reflect our fragmentation.

A new paradigm would show us plainly that one of the most striking evidences of art currently underway in our community is the lonely work of Anna Marie Blas Arceo. Amid the tired, decades-long lament about how our native tongue is on the verge of extinction, she is working dutifully to save it.[74] Such undertaking has proven a long road, as she has only a handful of co-workers and as few of us recognize or are concerned that language is the umbilical cord of culture and that it should therefore be among the first things we protect.[75] Only a couple of months ago we saw the fruit of her most recent labor in the opening of the *Hurao* summer camp, at which our children are learning everything from the language, plants, and all the uses of the coconut tree to weaving, chant, song, and history. What I see in this effort is something she has long told me – that change comes not by a hammer but by attraction. Her *modus operandi* is to cause the hearts of the young to become attracted. The greatest degree of their attraction, she tells me, is history. Once they know from where, from what values, from what kind of people they come, our children are inevitably attracted, drawn by an

---

74.   Among the younger generation, there are fewer and fewer of us able to speak the Chamoru language and many of us are legitimately concerned that it will die with our generation. To understand how this situation came to be, it helps to remember that this is tied to the long processes of socialization and assimilation in Guahan, both of which served the project of our Americanization. Among my parent's generation are many who considered teaching children the Chamoru language less important than teaching them English, as they considered the latter more capable of carrying them into successful futures. In addition, in a post WWII Guahan, Chamorus were punished for speaking the language and deeply impacted by colonial policies and attitudes that in essence told Chamorus that our ways and language were inferior to the ways and language brought here by the U.S.

75.   Her faithful co-workers include Theresa "Ewy" Taitano, Joseph Peredo, Irene S. Quidachay, Mariana Guzman, Victor Tuquero, Tom and Chris Concepcion, and Leonard Iriarte.

organic impulse to find a mirror in which their faces appear. If the rest of us could begin to discern the depth of this caliber of art, I have no doubt we'd help our sister Anna Marie realize her dream of opening an actual immersion school for our children to master our language. The building of a school would suggest that we remember the existence of another worldview, one filled with values that counter the consumerist, fraudulent ones dominating the intellectual landscape of the contemporary world.

We must push art into some bigger space. Even the sacred sound of *Guma' Pålu Li'e,'* which is literally re-opening an entry to a lost world, is not enough. What it does provide is an example of good art. Akin to womanism, it is art created for the good of the whole to make us whole, something that not just elates, but elevates. Forged from the sacred stone of reclaimed indigenous identity, it is art capable of penetrating the internalized colonization poisoning our lives, arming us as we march in from the margins. On a deeply personal level, it has given me something I have long yearned for, even if not entirely aware of it – a way to honor the women in my line. Indeed, "The House" has given me just that - a home in the knowledge that I come from a line of women who remain: A boy – who lost his father to cancer at nine years of age; who spent a childhood holding his grieving mother; and who would later come to see standing in uncompromising solidarity with the most disenfranchised women as the most critical choice he could ever make – not only found a home but came home.

Art that is worthy of our people must equip us with a fresh capacity to have more frank and loving conversations with each other as well as the humility to stay in it. It must help us live, and re-create community, polity, prayer.

Frankly what we need is to not drown. Our art, by consequence, must concern every single thing that will help prevent that from happening.

Artists arise. Bring forth your gifts so that all of us – not some – may survive.

Just Left of the Setting Sun

Our island home is on a collision course with history in this day and it is late in the day. Late enough that we have determined some important things: Fewer and fewer of our leaders are proving able to stand against the stinging forces of global politics and their diminished will has informed their complicity. The military industrial complex is etched into the entire landscape of their intentions and their actions profess they are still drunk with the promises of colonial favor. And though such things would see fit to defeat what is left of our disfigured persons, we know that we come from a line of strong women who organized a powerfully matrilineal society and consider this a blessing closer to us than our own jugular vein.

Perhaps it is youth that affords the faith in our ability to rise above our oppressed condition, but I suspect otherwise. Through chant and prayer, unfolding is an older understanding: if we could come into the awareness that our ancestors are neither absent nor far away, we could take from this the sustenance our souls so badly need. Such an understanding enables us to confront the callousness of a history needing us always to believe we are victims, not agents. What we must take from this collision is an opportunity to become the kind of people we want to be in the world. Today we must find the moral and spiritual center from which will flow a politics of resistance capable of heralding a new chapter in Guahan history, a people who participate in the design of their destiny.

People often ask where Guahan is headed, in this era of growing disparity between the poor and rich and ever more sophisticated justifications for human misery.

In the end, the fruit that has come of intense reflection about the situation of the indigenous people of Guahan is…both small and imperfect. But it is, nonetheless, a refutation of that dangerous notion that we should wait until all the answers are in before we walk in a given direction. To put it plainly, that idea is strangling us. The suggestion that we Chamorus should not move forward with an agenda for the recognition of our human rights without all the kinks worked out first is not only perilous; it is poisonous.

In my own interior journey, I have found that for the work of cultural revival and the pursuit of social justice in a political climate that insists on dehumanizing us, there is no blueprint – no plan so elaborately schemed it will surely meet success. To love freedom is to find a place within the struggle. The reality that there is no blueprint for justice work is not as forceful a fact as these: wrongs must still be righted; empowered people longing for wholeness have always waged the battle for freedom from the bottom of hills, not from on top of them; if compassion, not cleverness, is what informs our movement's vision, then our walking will be redemptive.

> O SON OF SPIRIT!
> The best beloved of all things in My sight is Justice; turn not away therefrom if thou desirest Me, and neglect it not that I may confide in thee. By its aid thou shalt see with thine own eyes and not through the eyes of others, and shalt know of thine own knowledge and not through the knowledge of thy neighbor. Ponder this in thy heart; how it behoveth thee to be. Verily justice is My gift to thee and the sign of My loving-kindness. Set it then before thine eyes.[76]

At 23, along with a promise of solidarity, I offer this:

Chamoru people: we must take back our stories. Our stories about who we are, what we value and honor, whom we love and how that love is made manifest. Such a move would help us begin decolonizing the colonial mentality that continues to contaminate our lives. Stories we have heard from the outside, stories about revolution and the politics of social change, keep telling us to keep our eye on the prize. What can we do with this? Do we keep our eye on the prize? On our still-denied right to Self Determination, for instance? Absolutely.

But if we could emancipate ourselves from the trappings of prevailing, individualistic thinking for one long and clear moment, I think we would intuitively figure out where to keep fixed our other eye – on each other, should one of us stumble. After all, we are a people and a people do not abandon their own. And should our pace be slowed, no matter. Because if we actually believe a beautiful redemption is on the horizon, at least for our children, each one of us will come to matter just

---

76.   From *The Hidden Words of Bahá'u'lláh*.

as much and more so than any one of our ideas of freedom, no matter how thoroughly crafted. We will come to understand, with the calm of a breeze through the heart, a simple truth: Our people deserve not only our patience and our understanding, but a painfully-borne commitment to continue trying to meet each other where we are at.

At the 9th annual Festival of the Pacific Arts in Belau in July of last year, the people of Guahan joined our sisters and brothers in one of the largest and most moving celebrations of cultural survival and pride in the Pacific Ocean. I was blessed to be among them. At a symposium on traditional navigation, I sat stunned listening to the sons of men who managed to hold on to an art I once believed dead. That day I rediscovered how a knowledge that was almost lost amid colonialism endured. Survived. In awe of these ordinary, these magnificent people, I felt as much at home as I ever had. Hours of dialogue ensued about how we, as Oceanic people, will successfully perpetuate the art of celestial navigation in an era when America's mass consumerist culture has already entered the psyche of our young people and is at every moment tightening its grip on the necks of their future. Elders cried, activists flared, scholars fidgeted in their seats at the expression of such deep and far-flung anguish; I came home into a painfully-earned awareness of how much we have lost and how much we stand to lose – an understanding that has forced me forever into adulthood.

One of the many things I learned that day was that in the old days our ancestors, to ensure their safe return home, would set their vessel just left of the setting sun. When the sun finally set, the light of the stars guided our way and brought us home.

In my quietest hour, I am freed by the faith that if we Chamorus of today could again be convinced to move in this direction, to allow our past to propel us forward, we would survive. Such an interruption in the status quo of colonial thinking disturbs the ease with which global politics are imposing its peril on our family members throughout the world.[77] This movement worries Empire. And it should. Because in the eleventh hour we can still prove that though we may be dormant, we are not dead yet. We have a gift our ancestors left us, a direction in which to set our *sakman*[78] of hope. If we can muster up the courage to trust in the old ways and take them as intellectually seriously as we do ways we have imported, I trust we would let the roots of our past inform the quality and color of our future.

We may not know all the nuances involved in successfully confronting four centuries of colonial dominance of our people, but we know we are being wronged. We may be without a blueprint, but we are not without vision. And ability.

If in the last estimation we are worthy of being elevated by the one God to the station of Servants Of Humanity, our walking will be upright. But by the rules of spiritual maturation, this must follow a prior kneeling, a genuflection in which we turn, with resolve, away from ego and self and vanity, and turn, with humility, toward the sublimity of that station. Only then can we find our feet and stand to shoulder a place in the sun of a newfound resplendency.

Fanoghe Chamoru.

77.　　For further decolonization literature focused on disrupting colonial thought and understanding cultural resistance as a response and counter-force to cultural hegemony, see Kay-Trask, Haunani (1999). *From a Native Daughter: Colonialism and Sovereignty in Hawaii*. See also Politics in the Pacific Islands: Imperialism and Native Self Determination from which the following quote is taken: "all Native cultural resistance is political; it challenges hegemony." For further reading on the movement to refocus and reframe academic research from Western approaches to non-Western methodologies, see (Maori) Smith, Linda Tuhiwai (1999). *Decolonizing Methodologies*.

78.　　Outrigger sailing canoe. The *sakman* is mentioned in essay 1 of this book, "The Emancipation of Morning".

Bibliography

Books

Bahá'u'lláh (1986). *The Arabic Hidden Words of Bahá'u'lláh.* Oxford, England: Oneworld Publications.

de Rivero, Oswaldo (2001). *The Myth of Development.* London: Zed Books.

Kay-Trask, Haunani (1999). *From a Native Daughter: Colonialism and Sovereignty in Hawaii.* Honolulu: University of Hawaii Press.

Lorde, Audre (1984). *Sister Outsider: Essays and Speeches.* Freedom, CA: The Crossing Press.

Nader, Ralph, Philips, David and Choate, Pat (1993). *The Case Against Free Trade: GATT, NAFTA, and the Globalization of Corporate Power.* San Francisco:Earth Island Press.

Neruda, Pablo (1993). *Twenty Love Poems and a Song of Despair.* New York:Penguin Classics.

Political Status Education Coordinating Commission (2002). *Kinalamten Pulitikåt: Siñenten I Chamorro: Issues in Guam's Political Development: The Chamorro Perspective.* Hagåtña, Guam: Political Status Education Coordinating Commission.

Roy, Arundhati (2001) *Power Politics*, Cambridge, Massachusetts: South End Press.

Smith, Linda Tuhiwai (1999). *Decolonizing Methodologies.* London: Zed Books.

Souder-Jaffery, Laura and Underwood, Robert ed. (1987). *Chamorro Self Determination: The Right of a People, I Derechon I Taotao.* Mangilao, Guam: Micronesian Area Research Center, University of Guam.

Walker, Alice (1983). *In Search Of Our Mother's Gardens: Womanist Prose*. New York: Harcourt Brace Jovanovich Publishers.

Paper Presentation

Teaiwa, Teresia (1992). Microwomen: US Colonialism and Micronesian Women Activists. Rubenstein, Donald, ed. *Pacific History: Papers from the 8ᵗʰ Pacific History Association Conference*. Mangilao, Guam: University of Guam and Micronesian Area Research Center. Pgs. 125-141.

Paper in Journal

Perez, Michael P. (2001). Contested Sites: Pacific Resistance in Guam to U.S. Empire. *Amerasia Journal* 27:1.

Internet Articles

Barlow, Maude and Clarke, Tony (2004 January). Water Privatization: The World Bank's Latest Market Fantasy. *Polaris Institute*.

Logan, Marty (2003 February) Multinationals Ride Wave of Water Privatization, Investigation Finds. *OneWorld US*.

Mann, Peter (2004) Water Wars: A Report from the World Social Forum [Electronic version].

Marsden, Bill (2003, February 3) Cholera and the Age of the Water Barons [Electronic version]. *The Center for Public Integrity*.

Public Citizen's Water for All Campaign online at <www.wateractivist.org>.

Salvador, Richard (1999, August). The Nuclear History of Micronesia and the Pacific. This article can be accessed online at < www.wagingpeace.org/articles/1999/08/00_salvador_micronesia.htm >.

Slattery, Kathleen (2003). What Went Wrong? Lessons from Cochabamba, Manila, Buenos Aires, and Atlanta *as part of Annual Privatization Report 2003, Reason Public Policy Institute.*

Newspaper Articles (Pacific Daily News)

Activists Worry, Officials Dispel Privatization Fears. (2005, June 14). *Pacific Daily News.* p. 3.

Critical Habitat Proposed. (2002, October 17) *Pacific Daily News.*

George Among Best of Gannett. (2002, May 12). *Pacific Daily News*, p. 2.

GWA Options Weighed (2004, May 22). *Pacific Daily News*, Section: Local.

Just Do It. (2005, May 28).*Pacific Daily News,* Section: Our View, p. 14.

Journals

White, Geoffrey M. & Lindstrom, Lamont (1993). Oceania: Islands, Land, People. *Cultural Survival Quarterly: State of the Peoples*, Issue 17.3.

Broadcasts

(2004, March 31), CBC broadcast. *The Fifth Estate: Dead in the Water, The World Bank: A Private-Sector Fix for a Public Water Crisis.*

Reports

Briscoe, Charles L.S. (author), Castro, William M. (editor), and Celestial, Robert N. (consultant) (2002, November 12) *The Blue Ribbon Panel Committee Action Report On Radioactive Contamination in Guam Between 1946-1958.* From the offices of Senator Angel L.G. Santos & Senator Mark Forbes. Hagåtña, Guam.

Glossary of Acronyms

Chamber of Commerce	COC
Consolidated Commission on Utilities	CCU
Government of Guam	GovGuam
Guam Waterworks Authority	GWA
International Financial Institution	IFI
International Monetary Fund	IMF
Non-Self-Governing Territory	NSGT
Organization of People for Indigenous Rights	OPIR
Pacific Daily News	PDN
People's Alliance for Dignified Alternatives	PADA
People's Alliance for Responsive Alternatives	PARA
Pacific Area Radiation Survivors	PARS
United Nations	U.N.
United States Department of Agriculture	USDA
U.S. Environmental Protection Agency	EPA
United States	U.S.
United States Department of Agriculture	USDA
World Bank	WB
World Trade Organization	WTO
World War II	WWII

Acknowledgements

This work would not have been possible without the unfailing love and support of:

My grandmother, the late Ana Roberto, and my father, the late Peter Perez Aguon, who have never left my side.

My sister Rhea for being for me that tower of support in everything I do. Without her, this book would have been but a dream deferred.

My mother Annabelle, who, by the sheer majesty of her resilience and integrity, has shown me since childhood what it means to be a servant of humanity. For giving me the gift of the knowledge that servitude is the highest station.

My other mother Cec, from whom I learned the most important lesson – humility. Like her art, she herself is a declaration of the presence of the beautiful and a testament to the truth that the greatest radiance is that of justice.

My other sister LisaLinda Natividad, the first to truly invite me to join her in becoming students of Chamoru culture and rights and then walked with me the whole way.

The community of the regal House of Chant that is *Guma' Pålu Li'e.'*

Sabina Flores Perez for her clear ray of morality shining like a sun on the landscape of our endeavors.

Rima Miles for her purity of heart, loving through the frustration.

Fanai Castro, my comrade and most careful editor.

Kelly Marsh for lending me her books, insight, encouragement, and ear.

Anne Perez Hattori and Leonard Iriarte for their scholarly and traditional guidance in this process.

Jill Benavente and Anna Marie Blas Arceo, who inspire me with the compassion that grounds their work and their lives.

Hoi Yin Chan for her cheerleading.

Bertha Guerrero and Tanya Champaco Mendiola, Chamoru women who never miss the forest for the tree.

My friends without whom I may not have survived my old university to make it home whole –

Cec Sheoships, Tennille Jeffries-Simmons, Rondesia Jarret.

And those who stood faithfully at our side –

The incomparable Jennifer McCarthy, who journeyed with me into India and into myself.

The soldier Sarah Sevedge, whose rage and tears keep the work real and pulsing.

The nobler of my teachers – Raymond Reyes, Tom Jeannot, Robert Prusch, Jeri Shepard, Bob Egan, Susan Foster-Dow.

Jane Rinehart, my most important professor, for walking with me into feminist, womanist, redemptive scholarship.

Erfana Dar of Kashmir, who was there in the beginning when this dawn was only breaking, and I just a fledgling to the light.

Ridhima Verma of India, my most feral of friends, on whose lashes I can always find refuge.

Brengyei Katosang of Belau, for getting me into gear with her signature tough love and enduring companionship.

Acknowledgements

Kat Gisog of Yap, for her sustaining affections.

Kanakolu Noa of Hawaii, who shared with me the struggle of the *kanaka maoli* before I came home to my own people.

Marie Santos, for safeguarding a space for me when I was young and had yet to come into my own.

Seeta, my tree, for coffee, luring me into literature, and reviewing my manuscript.

Those who saw promise in this project and encouraged it into reality – Tina Muña Barnes, Jaha Cummings and Lisa Baza.

Bob Marley and Alice Walker, two human beings I have never met but love fiercely, whose work has changed and saved my life and is medicine for our ailing world.

And, finally, women of color everywhere, who are and have always been my most noteworthy companions and teachers, at whose side I will stand until the victory is won.

Introducing *The Spiritual Traveler Series* from
blue ocean press

The Spiritual Traveler Series provides the reader with a new type of travel writing experience. Instead of simply looking at the sights, sounds, and tastes of a locale, the Spiritual Traveler allows the reader to experience the consciousness of a nation.

"The tourist takes in the sights; the traveler sees the reality of the landscape."

The Spiritual Traveler Vol. I
Cuba is a State of Mind
p.w. long
with
Juaquin Santiago and Elijo Truth

Excerpts from the essay *"Cuba is a State of Mind":*

What is it about Cuba that stimulates our senses, makes us yearn for more of her? What is the seemingly magical energy that permeates the soul of almost every Cuban? What is that infectious quality that can only be labeled "Cuban"?

If you truly allow yourself to partake of Cuba, sip from her cup, eat from her plate, take her in, you will never be the same. When you fully experience Cuba you must surrender, But once bitten, you cannot stay away, you must return. One thing is certain, you will not change Cuba - she will change you...

Cuba is a State of Mind - The Spiritual Traveler Vol. I, is also included in the 1898 Consciousness Studies Series by blue ocean press. These studies examine the consciousness of locales affected by the handover of Spanish territories to the U.S. after the Spanish-American War. These include Guahan (Guam), The Philippine Islands, Puerto Rico, and Cuba. These studies reveal similarities and differences in political and cultural consciousness between these countries and territories.

Year of Publication: 2006
ISBN: 978-4-902837-18-8
Softcover
Price $12.95

Other titles by blue ocean press coming out in 2007

The Spiritual Traveler Vol. II
Micronesia: The Good Life
p.w. long
ISBN: 978-4-902837-02-1

What is the "good life"? Is it a given or must we earn it? Must we give up something to get it? On her trip to Micronesia, Majuro (the Marshall Islands), Pohnpei, and Chuuk, the traveler pondered the meaning of the "good life". What better place on earth to consider this question than the these islands so bountifully blessed by nature. Upon reaching the Marshall Islands, the Pearl of the Pacific, the traveler is sure that on these islands, indeed the true good life is experienced. She is saddened however, to learn that many of the Marshallese have forsaken that life for a few deadly baubles; white sugar, flour, salt, and rice. The traveler experiences the incredible beauty of Pohnpei, the mysteries of Nan Madol, and partakes of Sakau, but is frustrated when she hears of the "miseducation" of the Micronesian children. Finally, the traveler is enthralled by the similarities between the Chuukese and the black people that she knew in the rural south. She sits for hours relishing the lagoon and watching boats speed to the outer islands. Again, however, she listens in dismay as she hears stories of the disintegration of the Chuukese extended family. As she leaves these idyllic islands, one agonizing question remains deep in the heart of the traveler. By whose standards do we judge the good life, and must we give up our identity, our cultural center, and our essence to have it, even if the definition is not our own?

The Spiritual Traveler Vol. III
New Orleans: The Essence of the Big Easy
p.w. long
ISBN: 978-4-902837-03-X

New Orleans has always been one of the traveler's favorite cities. Since she was a girl, she has loved the place. Her first memories of New Orleans are sitting on the porch of family friends and feasting on red beans and rice deep in the heart of the Ninth Ward. She has returned again and again, taking her children there so that they could experience the magic of this wonderful city.

The traveler even has a set of rituals reserved for her visits. She must stay at the St. James Hotel, a 1857 landmark, furnished in the French Indies style that she loves. Her first breakfast in the city is one of beignets and café au lait at the Café du Monde. She must have a shrimp po-boy at some time during her visit, and cannot leave the city without relishing the fried pickles from her favorite restaurant, The Praline Connection. A ride in a riverboat along the

Mississippi is mandatory and $20.00 played on the quarter slot machines at Harrad's completes the list of must do's.

New Orleans has a vibrancy, an energy, a presence of spirit that cannot be defined, only experienced. Being there feels almost surreal. New Orleans is a place to eat good food, have a good time, and even engage in excesses if you must. For many people who visit, it is a time to take off the mask, to let their dark side be known. The hedonism and extreme vulgarity so often exhibited by tourists attending Mardi Gras is evidence of this. Now in the aftermath of Hurricane Katrina, the dark side of New Orleans has come to light and the mask has been removed for the world to see. The traveler takes a deeper look at New Orleans; with and without her mask, so that the city's essence can be revealed.

How To Rule the World:
Lessons in Conquest for the Modern Prince
J.F. Cummings
ISBN: 978-4-902837-00-5

How to Rule the World is a modern adaptation of Machiavelli's *The Prince*. The author provides the reader, the Prince, with a methodology of non-invasive influence and control that will grant him sovereignty over his or her desired target nation-state and eventually over the world at large.

How To Rule the World shows the modern Prince how to utilize "modern ideals" such as free trade, democratic governance, human rights, freedom and individual rights, rule of law, and free press to exert control over other nations and convince them to collaborate in their own domination and exploitation through their quest to do whatever is required of them to be accepted as "developed", "modern" nations.

Through adherence to the methodology of conquest explained the book the Prince will be granted access to the psyche of the target nation's population and will be able to redefine its very sense of worth and self-definition. This book advises a Prince on what is necessary to create an empire based on the sustainable exploitation of targeted nations and what the cost of a mismanaged and irresponsible campaign can be to the targeted nations, his own nation, and the world-at-large.

How to Rule the World, is written in first-person like *The Prince*, and is a conversation with the reader, leading to self-examination his or her own value system, thought processes, and concepts of human nature. It provides a forum through which the reader can determine his or her position in the world and within their own psyche as 'Prince' or 'subject', and how the actions of both impact on the very sustainability of the human species.